MW01153393

GENERATION QUEER

STORIES OF YOUTH ORGANIZERS, ARTISTS, AND EDUCATORS

GENERATION QUEER

STORIES OF YOUTH ORGANIZERS, ARTISTS, AND EDUCATORS

Kimm Topping

illustrated by Anshika Khullar

TU BOOKS

An imprint of LEE & LOW BOOKS INC.

New York

Text copyright © 2025 by Kimm Topping
Cover art and interior illustrations copyright © 2025 by Anshika Khullar
Cover protest crowd silhouette by Nadya Ustuzhantceva/Adobe Stock
All rights reserved. No part of this book may be reproduced, transmitted,
or stored in an information retrieval system in any form or by any means,
electronic, mechanical, photocopying, recording, or otherwise, without written
permission from the publisher.

TU BOOKS, *an imprint of* LEE & LOW BOOKS INC.
381 Park Avenue South, New York, NY 10016
leeandlow.com

Printed in China by RR Donnelley

Edited by Stacy Whitman
Book design by Sheila Smallwood
Typesetting by ElfElm Publishing
Book production by The Kids at Our House
The text is set in Bryant
The illustrations were created digitally

10 9 8 7 6 5 4 3 2 1
First Edition

Cataloging-in-Publication Data can be found at the Library of Congress.
ISBN 978-1-64379-520-1 (HC)
ISBN 978-1-64379-521-8 (EBK)

The facts in the text were accurate and all hyperlinks were live at the time of
the book's original publication. The author and publisher do not assume any
responsibility for changes made since that time.

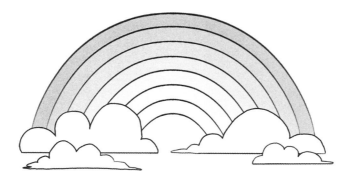

To the youth who are creating history
and reclaiming the future,

To every queer and trans person who
has struggled and persisted,

To the young activists who refuse to stay silent and
who pave the way for a more inclusive world,

To the quiet ones whose compassion and
self-expression are acts of activism,

To every version of yourself that you will
grow to love and appreciate,

To those who have been searching for a book like this—
may it remind you that you are always enough,

And in everything I do—for my brother.

—K. T.

· ·

For my mama, my first and fiercest ally.
I feel your pride, now and always; warm and eternal.

—A. K.

CONTENTS

INTRODUCTION 1

CHAPTER 1: ORGANIZERS 21

ANDRAYA YEARWOOD 40

CYN MACIAS-GÓMEZ 44

DEHKONTEE CHANCHAN 50

GAVIN GRIMM 53

KAYLYN AHN 57

L AUSTIN-SPOONER & KATHERINE FERREIRA
   O'CONNOR 62

LILLIAN LENNON 66

SHERENTÉ MISHITASHIN HARRIS 69

SKYLER MORRISON 73

ZANDER MORICZ 76

CHAPTER 2: ARTISTS 79

ALOK VAID-MENON 90

ELLA MCKENZIE 93

JESS GUILBEAUX 97

JOSHUA ALLEN 100

MEG LEE 103

REEVES GIFT 106

RYAN CASSATA 109

SARA K. DUNN 113

SHANNON LI 116

SOMAH HAALAND 120

CHAPTER 3: EDUCATORS 123

ASHTON MOTA 135

BLAIR IMANI 138

DESMOND (DESI) NAPOLES 141

JP GRANT 145

MALLERY JENNA ROBINSON 149

MARI WROBI 153

REBEKAH BRUESEHOFF 157

SAMEER HUSSAIN JHA 160

SCHUYLER BAILAR 164

TRINITY NEAL 167

CHAPTER 4: FROM WALKOUTS TO MARCHES: DEMANDING QUEER YOUTH SAFETY, AUTONOMY, AND JOY 169

CHAPTER 5: ACTIONS FOR YOUTH 185

CHAPTER 6: ACTIONS FOR EDUCATORS 203

ACKNOWLEDGMENTS 215

ABOUT THE AUTHOR 217

ABOUT THE ILLUSTRATOR 219

SOURCES 221

GENERATION QUEER

STORIES OF YOUTH
ORGANIZERS, ARTISTS,
AND EDUCATORS

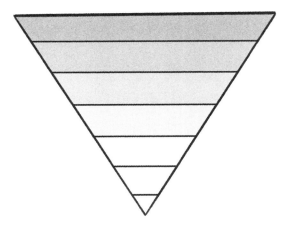

INTRODUCTION

What do you envision when you imagine a future in which all young people are thriving, safe, and able to achieve meaningful lives for themselves?

Allow yourself to dream for a moment beyond the limitations and barriers of oppression we face now. Think about what joy and authenticity mean for you, and what they look like in practice. Imagine how it would feel to experience classrooms, community centers, and homes in this future. Picture it and arrive there.

It doesn't take much imagination or far-fetched thinking to envision this world, considering that young people have the answers and have been shouting them for generations. The future that young people are creating the road map to is inclusive. It is a future where all of us can bring our full selves, languages, families, and histories into every space and relationship. There's no need to code-switch or suppress ourselves.

This future is anti-racist. It acknowledges that so much of humanity's collective knowledge is rooted in Black, Brown, and Indigenous communities, and all people of the global majority, and that reparations are owed to BIPOC communities. It is freed from genocide, ethnic cleansing, and all

WHAT DO YOU ENVISION WHEN YOU IMAGINE A FUTURE IN WHICH ALL YOUNG PEOPLE ARE THRIVING, SAFE, AND ABLE TO ACHIEVE MEANINGFUL LIVES FOR THEMSELVES?

forms of violence, while the truths of these harmful histories are not censored or erased. Stories representing all humanity are available.

This future is accessible for all neurodivergent and disabled youth—and systems are built by and for youth, not just with them in mind. Education is celebrated and everyone has access to the information they need, like comprehensive sexual health education. There are sustainable solutions to climate change and the harms of capitalism.

It is a future with safe, affirming homes—and access to housing for everyone. Access to basic human needs, like food, clean water, and healthcare, is abundant. This time we're envisioning is free from gun violence, police brutality, and sexual assault. This future is safe, loving, and made possible through collective forms of care. It's transformative and creative. This is the future the youth featured in this book—and so many others—are working toward.

This book is a love letter to the many generations of queer and trans youth who have committed their time and energy to demanding a better future for themselves and for humanity. They have thoughtfully and intentionally built upon the legacies of so many trans and queer ancestors before them in order to bring that vision much closer to the present tense. It is also a commitment from older generations: we will partner with Gen Z and Gen Alpha; we will not just stand on the sidelines and say, "The youth will save us."

As you read the stories collected here, I hope you'll be reminded of the many ways we can celebrate the past, create the present, and envision the future. This book is an affirmation that there are so many people like you imagining similar solutions. An assurance that you are not alone, and never have been. A call to action to respond fearlessly to the legislation and systems that seek to erase us, and to create and build better ones instead. A promise that there is care and love for you in this world—and for so many people like you who share in your longing for a better future.

Generation Queer is the first collection of illustrated biographies about queer and trans youth who are leaders in social change. From Trinity Neal celebrating self-expression and family in her first book, *My Rainbow*, to grassroots organizer Lillian Lennon advocating for trans leadership in Alaska, to Sameer Jha providing education to teachers across the country, and many more, these young people are shifting cultural stereotypes about who is allowed to lead. This book is all about the brilliant and compassionate leadership of current queer and trans youth activists. It's a celebration of how youth today are applying *queer* as a verb—as in: queering education, organizing, and the arts. These are the three types of activism we'll explore in *Generation Queer*. Young people are creating a culture of radical self-expression, community care, and meaningful social change.

Each story shows us what can happen when young people lead—with a megaphone, with their camera, or at the front of the classroom. Their stories deserve a spotlight, and while they have many accomplishments to come as they grow, we should not wait until later to celebrate them. The contributions of youth are meaningful and worth our attention, especially right now.

GETTING HERE

Though I didn't start writing this book until 2018 (when I was twenty-five), it's the one I've been looking for since I was a young person—and one I've been creating in practice through my career as a youth worker and community organizer for more than ten years. When I came out in the seventh grade as a lesbian (and later discovered that I'm bisexual), I had several incredibly supportive friends and family members, and a few teachers who offered caring advice. However, the guidance counselor I confided in told my parents that I was likely going through a phase and

INVITING IN

"Coming out" was the phrase I heard a few times during brief glimpses of short films I caught on LOGO (a gay television network). I'd turn it on late at night or when my family wasn't home, because it was the only place I could find media about LGBTQIA+ people, and I wanted to understand myself.

The **National Black Justice Coalition** uses the term **"inviting in"** to describe sharing our queerness, which shifts the expectation and clarifies that no one is owed access to information about people's identities or relationships. Has anyone ever had to "come out" as straight or cisgender? Absolutely not! It's unfair that there is this imbalance in power and expectations.

We invite others in to see our full lives and selves. We welcome them wholeheartedly to see us as full people, and they decide how to accept that invitation. Who we are is not a secret or something to be ashamed of—though it's understandable that many of us struggle with these feelings. It is incredible when we share our full selves, and it should be celebrated.

could be changed. It had taken me several months of certainty, following many years of questioning, to find the right words to share this part of my identity with my parents. So it was a big deal when I decided to share this truth with them. I had hoped that this guidance counselor would be equipped to convey to my family that being queer is not only normal, but also just one piece of the full person they already knew.

Because of the stigma we often experience, it is a common feeling among queer and trans people that reaching adulthood feels like a miracle. It certainly did for me. Young people deserve much more than the bare minimum of survival. They deserve thriving futures. We all deserve to see our lives as valuable, brilliant, fulfilling, and worth living.

The day I shared my truth with my family was well after Massachusetts became the first state in the country to amend its student anti-discrimination law, protecting students from discrimination on the basis of sexuality, in 1993, the year I was born. Of course, laws are only one solution, and it takes time to shift and influence ingrained societal messages. When a guidance counselor betrayed my trust and enforced beliefs that my family had long been taught to uphold, I felt alone and didn't know how to ask for help. When I was growing up, I didn't have a book or a television show about people like me—LGBTQIA+ youth who wanted to fight for a better future.

I did have friends who shared this passion and faced the same questions and roadblocks. We'd dream together about moving to New York City (the only place where we knew queer people were out and visible), but we didn't have access to local role models or mentors who would answer our toughest questions. I didn't know an openly queer adult until my early

ALLOW YOURSELF TO **DREAM** FOR A MOMENT **BEYOND THE LIMITATIONS** AND BARRIERS OF **OPPRESSION** WE FACE NOW.

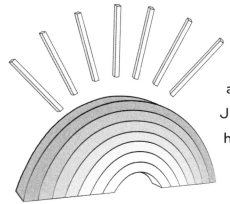

twenties. I didn't know the word *transgender* until I reached college and read a book by a trans author for the first time, *Redefining Realness* by Janet Mock. Reading about the trans experience helped me learn the terminology that I needed to describe myself when I had heard only derogatory slurs aimed at the community before then.

We turned to musicians who embraced gender fluidity for inspiration. I was definitely an emo kid fascinated by My Chemical Romance defying gender and sexuality norms in their music videos and performances. I didn't know how to find helpful resources online or in my local community, so any signifiers of queerness stood out to me. I had no idea that young people like me were marching to the State House to demand better protections for us.

If I had seen students in my own state rewriting the law through their advocacy, I would have joined them! Or at the very least, I would

GAVIN GRIMM

have felt seen. If I had known the stories of young people like Gavin Grimm—a high school student from Virginia who advocated for full access to his education, took his case all the way to the Supreme Court, and won; or Dehkontee Chanchan—a housing advocate who finds safe homes for queer and trans youth—I might have had a better sense of my own ability to influence change earlier.

Years after those difficult days of figuring out how I could invite others in, I started the first Gender-Sexuality Alliance (GSA) in my town. Even then, I didn't know that I had rights as a queer young person to start a GSA in my public school (more on this in chapter 3), but I felt the need to do something. Many young people are still in that same position, unaware of their rights until they need to advocate for themselves or their friends.

What would a future look like where all queer and trans young people are empowered with the education and tools to understand the possibilities available to them, as well as their ability to lead within their communities?

As an educator, I can work directly with LGBTQIA+ youth to support their leadership and advocacy work, as well as coach school staff on creating classrooms that are LGBTQIA+ inclusive. I even had the opportunity to return to my high school and support student leaders with hosting an equity conference through History UnErased, an educational nonprofit promoting LGBTQ visibility and representation in history, civics, and social studies education. Now, my high school has a thriving GSA and even more caring educators advocating for them. It was a full-circle moment and a reminder that change is happening. Sometimes it's incremental and sometimes it's large-scale. It's especially effective when it's led by young people themselves.

On the days when I feel most present, I am honored to be the needed queer adult that my younger self lacked. I wrote this book as a tool youth and educators may use to continue their important work toward the future they're dreaming of.

There are a few things that I think are important to know from anyone who is writing about history, living people, and our communities that I want to share here before we get to the rest of the book.

QUEER AS A VERB

The title of this book might make you wonder "Hmm, are you trying to say this is the *first* generation that's queer?" Absolutely not! We've been here forever. What this book aims to do is highlight the way that particular generations—Gen Alpha, Gen Z, and Millennials—approach advocacy. Throughout the book, I'll use the word *queer* as an umbrella term to describe ways of thinking, doing, and existing that defy the norms set out to control or restrict our ways of being. Colonization and systems of oppression have institutionalized ideologies that harm queer people, particularly BIPOC queer communities. Queering is about rethinking and reimagining, while also acknowledging our true histories that have been erased or ignored.

Saying someone or something is queer doesn't necessarily tell you anything about gender or sexuality (though it can), and that's what people find so freeing about it. And yet it's a term that also holds a painful history for many. It's been reclaimed by some from what was once a derogatory slur for people like us (and still can be when used to cause harm or violence), so it's important to be mindful of the differences between *queer* as a verb, as an umbrella term for the community, and as a label for someone's identity. What matters is that we reflect back the language people use for themselves. People get to decide what language they use for themselves that best describes their own experiences. Building an intergenerational movement means meeting people where they're at, acknowledging their perspective, and respecting it.

"OFTEN WE SEE QUEERNESS AS A DEPRIVATION, BUT WHEN I LOOK AT MY LIFE, I SAW THAT QUEERNESS DEMANDED AN ALTERNATIVE INNOVATION FROM ME, I HAD TO MAKE ALTERNATIVE ROUTES. IT MADE ME CURIOUS, IT MADE ME ASK—THIS IS NOT ENOUGH FOR ME BECAUSE THERE'S NOTHING HERE FOR ME."
—OCEAN VUONG, AUTHOR OF *ON EARTH WE'RE BRIEFLY GORGEOUS* (2019)

"On an individual level, I understand there is a lot of utility in using the word *queer*. It's a catch-all term. I don't particularly like using the word *queer*. I think of a few different things—a very hateful word. When I think of queerness, I think of something that's very dynamic and flexible and very changing. I am none of those things. I actually feel really uncomfortable in queer spaces, a unique problem a lot of masculine people feel. We've determined that masculine people are capable of taking pain. Black women are perceived as masculine. In heteronormative and queer spaces, we see that repeated. Men seen as not having feelings. It re-creates a harmful cycle of stoicism."

REEVES GIFT

—Reeves Gift, artist (see chapter 2)

There are so many terms that folks use to capture our community in its fullness, like 2SLGBTQIA+, which represents Two-Spirit, lesbian, gay, bisexual, transgender, queer, questioning, intersex, asexual, aromantic, and many other ways of describing gender identity, gender expression, and sexual orientation. PBS's Map of Gender-Diverse Cultures (pbs.org/independent lens/content/two-spirits_map-html) is one place you can learn about the diversity of experiences around the world.

Pro tip: When someone shares their identity with you, you can ask "What does that mean for you?" to learn more about how they define it. This shows that you're curious, caring, and willing to learn. It also shows you're aware that these terms have more than one definition and are frequently expanding and being updated as people learn more about themselves, their histories, and the possibilities of language.

You may also see QTBIPOC (queer and trans Black and Indigenous people of color), LGBTQIA+, queer and trans, and other iterations. I'll use all interchangeably throughout—sometimes specific to a resource

I'm referencing—and I'll always attempt to respect the language that is used directly by the youth who were interviewed. There isn't a single agreement in the community about which terminology to use as the umbrella term, which is why I'll use a range of initialisms through-out. Language is always shifting and adapting as we gain greater access to understanding humanity, so we can expect that even more terminology will likely be used by the time of the publication of this book.

WE'RE THE EXPERTS OF OUR OWN EXPERIENCE

We all have so much more learning to do and always will. I cannot (and won't) speak on behalf of the entire queer and trans community. No one can, and we shouldn't try to! I'm the expert of my own experience, just like you are of yours. I am a white, queer, trans, genderfluid, disabled, chron-ically ill, English-speaking, first-generation college-educated person who is a settler on the stolen lands of the Pawtucket and Massachusett people. All these experiences impact how I understand the world and have influ-enced the histories I've learned, and what I need to unlearn. Namely, my whiteness often shields me and offers me privileges, despite the other marginalized identities that I hold. Committing to anti-racist work and learning is a lifelong endeavor. In the words of Ericka Hart, a racial, social, and gender justice educator, "Your queerness does not absolve your racism."

I never learned LGBTQIA+ history as a young person—in fact, there were eighteen years of my life during which I didn't have the opportunity

The term "Two-Spirit" was established in 1990 during the Third Spiritual Gathering of Gay and Lesbian Native People in Winnipeg, Manitoba, Canada. Elder Myra Laramee first introduced the term, translating the Anishinaabemowin word "niizh manidoowag," which means "two spirits." Activist Albert McLeod helped further develop the term to encompass Indigenous individuals within the LGBTQ community who hold traditional third-gender roles. The term aimed to distinguish Indigenous gender and sexuality concepts from those of non-Native LGBTQ people and to replace pejorative anthropological terms. This was finalized over five conferences, culminating in 1990, to ensure the recognition and inclusion of Indigenous LGBTQ identities in contemporary discussions, particularly during Pride Month and Indigenous History Month.

to learn our history at all. Much of the history I did have the opportunity to learn earlier in life was from a white masculine perspective. This is an example of whitewashing, which Desi Napoles talks about in chapter 3.

In my senior year of high school, I scoured the library for any story I could possibly find about queer and trans people with the goal of creating a research project focused on LGBTQIA+ history. I could find only one sentence: in a textbook about the 1960s that mentioned the Stonewall Inn riots, but without in-depth context about the overlapping injustices of racism, classism, and cis-heteronormativity that led to the riots.

This is just one example of the many challenges we're aiming to address: a lack of LGBTQIA+ inclusion in curriculum and education. While I've made every effort to learn our history as an adult, that gap means that I am continuously learning and have much more to explore. We all do—we're lifelong learners! I can't wait to learn from all of you—the readers—as this book makes its way into schools, youth centers, and homes, and as discussion of this book makes its way onto social media.

The stories of the youth featured in *Generation Queer* came from interviews, followed by feedback directly from each person to make sure that what was written reflected their experience. As the book is shared publicly, each of the young people will speak for themselves about their story. I invite you to learn directly from them. Follow their social media, learn about the organizations they're leading, and read other interviews or projects they've participated in. Many of us doing this work and sharing our stories publicly are facing negative pushback online and in public spaces, and we need your visible support to counter that. Livelihoods, safety, and well-being are actively being threatened by anti-LGBTQIA+ efforts.

A NOTE ON "FIRSTS"

You'll notice throughout timelines and stories in *Generation Queer* that there is some celebration of people being the "first"' to accomplish something within their identity group(s). I want to be clear that someone becoming a "first" as a BIPOC, LGBTQIA+, disabled, or otherwise marginalized person is not a reflection of any lack of excellence and brilliance within those individuals and communities. Instead, what it reveals is a system that has historically and presently excluded people and created intentional roadblocks to their success. So when you see these "firsts," I hope you'll get curious about what barriers prevented these milestones from happening sooner.

Can you find more examples of excellence in a particular field? What hidden stories are behind the accomplishments of someone who is the "first"? Who came before them or supported them?

FOLLOW YOUR CURIOSITY

Think of this book as a curiosity guide. You'll notice that names of people, organizations, and events; certain terms; and questions for reflection are set in boldface throughout the book.

This is a reminder for you to follow your curiosity! Never heard of STAR House before (see chapter 1)? Take a break from reading and see where a search leads you. Each chapter starts with a question to get you thinking about the things the youth in that chapter are advocating for. If you have a journal or somewhere else to write your thoughts down while reading, you can take some time to reflect at the start of the chapter, and then at the

ORAL HISTORY PROJECTS

ACT UP ORAL HISTORY PROJECT (actuporalhistory.org) is an archival collection of interviews with members of the AIDS Coalition to Unleash Power (ACT UP) in New York City.

LGBTQ RELIGIOUS ARCHIVES NETWORK (lgbtqreligiousarchives.org) is an oral history project with interviews of more than sixty early leaders of LGBTQ+ religious movements.

MAKING GAY HISTORY (makinggayhistory.com) highlights the hidden history of the LGBTQ civil rights movement through its podcast and educational materials.

NYC TRANS ORAL HISTORY PROJECT (nyctransoralhistory.org) is a community archive, organized in collaboration with the New York Public Library, documenting the voices of New York City trans people.

To find more oral history projects, you can visit the **LGBTQ Oral History Digital Collaboratory** (lgbtqdigitalcollaboratory.org), which has the largest digital history hub in North America for LGBTQ oral history.

MAP OF QUEER ARCHIVES

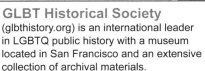

GLBT Historical Society (glbthistory.org) is an international leader in LGBTQ public history with a museum located in San Francisco and an extensive collection of archival materials.
San Francisco, CA

Gay and Lesbian Archive of Mid-America (libweb.umkc.edu /glama) is a collection representing the histories of LGBT communities in the Kansas City region.
Kansas City, MO

ONE Institute (oneinsTucson, AZ AZ) is the largest national repository of LGBTQ materials. They also host Youspeak Radio, an audio project led by youth.
Los Angeles, CA

Arizona Queer Archives (azqueerarchives.org) is a community-focused archival collection held at the Institute for LGBT Studies at the University of Arizona.
Tucson, AZ

The Queer Joy Project of East Texas (queerjoyetx.com) includes interviews with queer East Texans about their lives and what brings them joy.
Texas

National Deaf LGBT Archives (planet.deafqueer.com) is an extensive archive of Deaf queer art, oral history, writings, and more.
Virtual

AND ORAL HISTORY PROJECTS

The History Project (historyproject
.org) is the only organization focused on
documenting and preserving the history of
New England's LGBTQ communities.
Boston, MA

**LGBT Community Center
National History Archive**
(gaycenter.org/archives) is a community-
based archive housed at the NYC LGBT
Community Center that documents
LGBTQ lives and organizations centered
in and around New York City.
New York, NY

**Gerber/Hart Library and
Archives** (gerberhart.org)
focuses its collections on the
Chicago metropolitan area and
the Midwest. They operate a free,
public lending library representing
the histories of LGBTQ+ people.
Chicago, IL

**Sexual Minorities
Archives**
(sexualminoritiesarchives
.org) is one of the oldest
and largest collections
of LGBTQIA+ historical
documents, media, and
artifacts in the world.
Holyoke, MA

**NYC LGBT Historic Sites
Project** (nyclgbtsites.org) is a scholarly
initiative and educational resource that in
1994 helped create the nation's first map
for LGBT historic sites.
New York, NY

Lesbian Herstory Archives
(lesbianherstoryarchives.org) is the
world's largest collection of materials
by and about lesbians and their
communities.
Brooklyn, NY

Invisible Histories Project
(invisiblehistory.org) preserves an
accessible collection of the rich and
diverse history of LGBTQ life in the
US South.
**Alabama, Mississippi,
Georgia**

**Stonewall National
Museum, Archive, &
Libraries** (stonewall-museum
.org) is one of the largest gay
archives and libraries in the
United States.
Fort Lauderdale, FL

WHAT IS **YOUR DEFINITION OF LEADERSHIP? HOW DO YOU** RECOGNIZE **THE** LEADERS IN YOUR LIFE?

end of the chapter, see how your thoughts have shifted or expanded based on the stories you've read.

To learn even more, you can visit a national queer archive or a local archive in your town to see what you can find about queer history (see map on pages 14–15). Many archives have a digital collection that you can search online. Reach out to a local community organizer who can introduce you to activists in your area. Who is documenting their stories? You might even become a community historian yourself by following your interests and asking questions. There is endless queer and trans history for us to learn—because we have always been here and will always be here—and we need more people to record, uplift, and teach that history. Maybe you're making your own history in your town or school, a history that future generations of queer youth and others will be eager to learn.

LEADERSHIP IS EXPANSIVE

The movement is not, and never has been, led by a single person. The traditional model of leadership often highlights one person—the most extroverted, bold leader. Countless leaders have also been erased from our history books or silenced through criminalization and oppression. This means it's important that we not only uncover and acknowledge those stories but also question the dominant stories we've learned in the first place. Whether that's in a text you're reading for school, or something you see on social media, take a moment to pause and ask who is being centered in that narrative and why.

Movements need a whole lot of people with a common purpose and a willingness to learn from and with one another. While this book highlights a group of individual activists, it also aims to uplift the many histories of individuals, organizations, and communities through the introductory sections of each chapter, and the concluding three chapters. While those who are the first, or a founder, or the face of an action are integral to the success of our movements, it's so important to acknowledge everyone's contributions and all styles of leadership, including quiet leaders. Much like gender and sexuality, leadership is expansive, and there are so many ways to define it.

What is your definition of leadership? How do you recognize the leaders in your life?

BUILDING TRUST

You might wonder "Why isn't [insert awesome person] included?!" There are many people who I wanted to include in this book but ultimately did not for a number of reasons. Most important to me was the consent and enthusiasm of each person being included in a book like this one. If it wasn't an enthusiastic yes, I respected their choice. Trust is built and it is mutual. It is incredibly meaningful to me, and a real honor, that the young people featured in this book trusted me to write about their stories. Having your story shared publicly is an enormous responsibility, especially given the political climate and the attacks on LGBTQIA+ youth. For educators and other adults reading this book, this is a reminder that LGBTQIA+ youth should be celebrated and given space to share their voices, and at the same time, this should not be the expectation. Everyone deserves agency in making decisions about what and how much they share of themselves and their lives.

To narrow the focus, everyone featured in this book is currently based in the United States and started their activism before the age of twenty-four. The timelines and historical narratives are also US-based, so I encourage you to seek out more global resources and continue your learning. It's also important to keep in mind that the stories shared here are simply a snapshot in time of the many accomplishments and experiences each of the young people will have to share in their lifetime. Our identities can be fluid and can change over time— so names, pronouns, and words folks use to describe themselves may shift after the publication of this book, and that needs to be honored and respected. Some of the organizers, artists, and educators featured are well into their adulthood, yet the foundation of their activism started in childhood, so I felt it was important to include them.

Now that you have a sense of the vision for this book and what it hopes to accomplish, it's time to meet the youth organizers, artists, and educators of *Generation Queer*. In each chapter, you'll learn a bit of history about the three major topics through stories and timelines before reading about each activist. I've also included tons of resources to learn more in-depth histories.

CAN YOU FIND MORE EXAMPLES OF EXCELLENCE IN A PARTICULAR FIELD? WHAT HIDDEN STORIES ARE BEHIND THE ACCOMPLISHMENTS OF SOMEONE WHO IS THE "FIRST"?

You'll notice that, in chapter 1, the introduction about organizers is quite lengthy. I hope this gives you useful context for the movement as a whole and sets the stage for the chapters to follow. We'll bring it all together in chapter 4 to see how organizers, artists, and educators unify to protest.

In the final two chapters, you'll find resources for youth followed by resources for educators, including books and national organizations. Obviously, these aren't mutually exclusive, so check them all out.

Remember, follow your curiosity. And out of everything you'll learn from this book, one message is most important: Listen to LGBTQ youth and trust in their passionate, effective leadership. Onward!

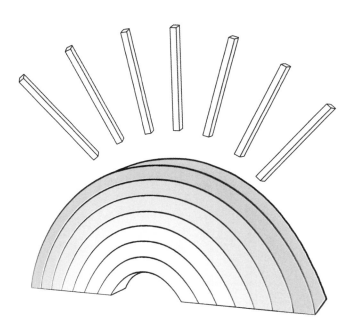

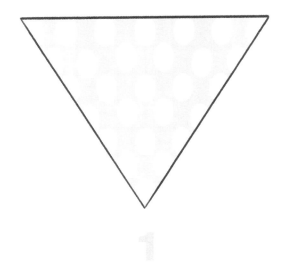

1

ORGANIZERS

What issues are you most passionate about? Do you know of local community organizers in your neighborhood who are speaking out about those topics? Can you think of a time when you inspired others to get involved with an important movement or cause?

Many of the young people here became organizers out of necessity. Denied rights, they felt compelled to speak up, not only for themselves but also for everyone else with shared experiences of oppression. By connecting intentionally with their communities, they found ways to create change. Some of the activists here never expected to speak publicly or to impact millions of people with their story. In fact, some still wouldn't label themselves as activists. They feel that they're simply doing what is right. The driving force of each of the youth featured here is the desire to have a future—for themselves and for all other individuals and generations that might come up against the same bigotry, invisibility, or discrimination.

They are community organizers building on generations of grassroots organizing and community mobilization. These young people are designing solutions and movements with the vision of a liberated, imaginative, and expansive future at the center of their work. Whether assembling resources for housing, arranging access to bath-room and public accommodations, organizing for Indigenous communities, securing protections for survivors of sexual assault, or protesting for safety from gun violence, these young people are advocating for themselves and all others being denied access to rights and opportunities.

WHAT IS A COMMUNITY ORGANIZER?

A community organizer creates collective action toward a common goal, often challenging policies or unfair treatment that targets particular groups of people. Organizers build relationships, inspire others to get involved, and, of course, they organize! They write op-eds, design flyers, make calls, create social media campaigns, call elected officials, create long-term plans, host community forums, train safety marshals for protests, and so much more. **Jamie Margolin**, a Colombian American climate justice activist and filmmaker, wrote a book about how young people can get involved in organizing titled *Youth to Power: Your Voice and How to Use It* (2020), which features interviews and helpful guides on how to get started.

WE'VE ALWAYS BEEN HERE

People have fought fearlessly—both publicly in the streets and in courthouses, and privately in their communities and families—to secure protections for LGBTQIA+ people. From access to public space to freedom from discrimination and violence, from a right to an education to the freedom of speech and protest, these are essential rights that have been denied to marginalized groups throughout history. The long history of resistance—by

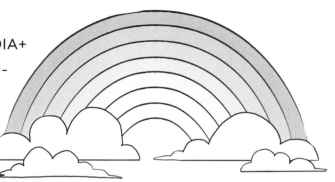

Black and Brown people, LGBTQIA+ people, disabled people, immigrants, Indigenous people, and low-income families—informs how the current generation of activists demand their rights.

An expansive range of genders, sexualities, and expressions have been around since the beginning of human history, though society's perception and treatment of us has ranged from loving and celebratory all the way to hateful and discriminatory. People across the gender spectrum exist and thrive across the globe, from Two-Spirit (Indigenous North America) to hijra (South Asia) to māhū (Hawaii and Tahiti) to fa'afafine and fa'afatama (Samoa) to xochihua (Central Mexico) to muxe' (Southern Mexico) to omeggid (Panama) and many more. There are LGBTQIA+ people in every culture, religion, and place, and there are accepting people everywhere too.

The roots of anti-LGBTQIA+ bias can be traced back to colonization and white supremacy. Eurocentric ways of thinking led to laws, penal codes, and ordinances restricting the expression of gender and sexuality. When we encounter examples of homophobia and transphobia, it's important to examine the roots and origins to fully understand the history, and to avoid stigmatizing particular cultures or communities for discrimination that didn't necessarily start with their beliefs.

EACH **PERSON** ATTRIBUTES **THEIR SUCCESS** TO THE **STRENGTH OF THEIR COMMUNITY,** RATHER THAN **EMPHASIZING** THEIR INDIVIDUAL **ACHIEVEMENT.**

SAMEER JHA

"I sometimes felt when I started out with activism that I was having to choose between being in South Asian spaces where my ethnicity and my culture was validated, and being in queer spaces where my queer identities were validated, but it was hard for me to exist with both simultaneously. I wanted to try to really bridge that gap and something that I found in doing that was that South Asia has a long history of celebrating and accepting queer and trans identities. South Asia actually has better trans laws than a lot of Europe and the Americas. It was really colonization that brought a lot of the ideologies that I think both South Asians and the West kind of think of as being inherent to South Asia. But really, that is a recent development. Reconnecting with some of that queer history has been really validating for me, that I can look back at documents and paintings from the 1600s and see myself represented, because that's not something I can really ever do with a lot of general queer media that focuses on America or the UK and mostly white people. So for finding that bridge between these different identities and feeling validated in all of them, it's been a journey . . . I'm so happy to discover this long history of acceptance."

—Sameer Jha, educator (chapter 3)

MOTHERS OF THE MOVEMENT

Youth have long been at the forefront of political action, protest, and community organizing. At the Stonewall Inn riots and uprising of 1969, one of the pivotal actions that led to the modern LGBTQIA+ rights movement, Marsha "Pay It No Mind" Johnson was twenty-three years old, and Sylvia Rivera was seventeen.

Marsha P. Johnson and Sylvia Rivera were two activists, and self-proclaimed drag queens, whose own experiences of homelessness, survival sex work, and discrimination led them to advocate for youth like themselves. Alongside Bubbles Rose Marie, they founded Street Transvestite Action Revolutionaries (STAR) and opened STAR House in New York City, which became the first LGBTQ+ youth shelter in North America.

In 1973, Sylvia Rivera gave a speech (sometimes referred to as the "Y'all Better Quiet Down" speech) at the Christopher Street Liberation Day Rally, where she called on gay and feminist activists to see her humanity—and to turn their energy to those most oppressed within the community, especially those experiencing homelessness, incarceration, sexual violence, and poverty.

LGBTQIA+ activists have not always been united in common goals.

"ON A HOT NIGHT IN JUNE 1969, POLICE RAIDED THE STONEWALL INN IN GREENWICH VILLAGE, NEW YORK, BUT THIS TIME RATHER THAN BE ARRESTED, THE QUEENS AND STREET KIDS FOUGHT BACK. THE RIOTS THAT ENSUED ARE CONSIDERED THE BEGINNING OF THE LGBTQ MOVEMENT IN AMERICA, BUT THE MOVEMENT HAS MUCH DEEPER ROOTS."

—LAVERNE COX NARRATING "TIME MARCHES FORWARD & SO DO WE" PRESENTED BY THE ACLU

Much of what we know about Sylvia Rivera and Marsha P. Johnson's legacies is thanks to Tourmaline, an activist and filmmaker who digitized records of their lives. Tourmaline directed and produced *Happy Birthday, Marsha!*, a film about Marsha P. Johnson's life, as well as "The Personal Things," a short film about Miss Major Griffin-Gracy, another visionary from the Stonewall Riots. Miss Major is an activist who has fought for the trans community for decades, particularly Black trans women and sex workers, and she is considered another mother of the movement. Documented by Toshio Meronek, Miss Major's life is told through interviews in *Miss Major Speaks: Conversations with a Black Trans Revolutionary* (2023).

Though transgender people have experienced the most marginalization and violence, some organizers within the movement have not always prioritized their leadership and calls for action, and focused on what they saw as more immediately achievable goals like marriage equality. Of course, this is an oversimplified explanation, so I encourage you to research the specific politics of each activist or group that has advocated for LGBTQ+ liberation. There are so many examples of multiracial, intergenerational, trans-inclusive organizations that we'll explore throughout the book.

The Stonewall Inn is a National Historic Landmark that still exists today as a public bar in New York City. In 1999, it became the first US site associated with LGBT civil rights to be listed on the National Register of Historic Places. A collection of archival documents related to Stonewall was released as a book by the New York Public Library in 2019, titled *The Stonewall Reader*. With the opening of the Stonewall National Monument Visitor Center in June 2024, the two parts of the original Stonewall Inn (51 and 53 Christopher Street) were reunited in purpose—though kept as separate spaces—for the first time since the riots, becoming the first LGBTQ+ focused visitor center in the US National Parks System.

BOOKS ABOUT LGBTQIA+ HISTORICAL FIGURES

A CHILD'S INTRODUCTION TO PRIDE: The Inspirational History and Culture of the LGBTQIA+ Community | Sarah Prager, Black Dog & Leventhal, 2023.

THE DEVIANT'S WAR: The Homosexual vs. The United States of America | Eric Cervini, Farrar, Straus and Giroux, 2020.

MODERN HERSTORY: Stories of Women and Nonbinary People Rewriting History | Blair Imani, Ten Speed Press, 2018.

QUEER HEROES: Meet 53 LGBTQ Heroes from Past and Present! | Arabelle Sicardi, Wide Eyed Editions, 2019.

A QUEER HISTORY OF THE UNITED STATES FOR YOUNG PEOPLE | Michael Bronski, Beacon Press, 2019.

SEEING GENDER: An Illustrated Guide to Identity and Expression | Iris Gottlieb, Chronicle Books, 2019.

TRANS AMERICA: A Counter-History | Barry Reay, Policy, 2020.

TRANSGENDER HISTORY | Susan Stryker, Seal Press, 2008.

EARLY ORGANIZING

Some of the earliest protests for gay and trans rights took place in spaces like restaurants or bars where people would gather for sanctuary. During these decades, it was illegal in many places to serve alcohol to "homosexuals," or even to someone suspected of being gay, and also for anyone to wear items of clothing that didn't "match" the sex assigned on their driver's license. Police would regularly raid local bars and restaurants frequented by LGBTQ+ people—arresting them, causing physical altercations, and making homophobic or transphobic comments. Queer and trans people fought back against these injustices of police brutality.

People would simply be living their lives and expressing themselves when police brutality, imprisonment, and violence would interrupt that. Communities needed to fight back, especially for those dually oppressed by racism and anti-LGBTQ bias. Riots, as Martin Luther King Jr. said, are the "language of the unheard." Because so few people outside the LGBTQ+ community understood or were willing to listen to their requests to respect their rights, queer people had to stand up in louder ways. The first documented riot in a public space by LGBTQ+ people was at Cooper Donuts in Los Angeles in 1959. This was followed by riots and sit-ins at Dewey's Restaurant in Philadelphia (1965), Compton's Cafeteria in San Francisco (1966), and Black Cat Tavern in Los Angeles (1967). These early riots set the foundation for what would be the gay liberation movement in the 1970s.

The word *homosexual* has a complicated history, much like the word *queer*. While many have claimed it for themselves, it has also been used to stigmatize people. It is a term that in the past was classified as a mental illness. Up until 1969, homosexuality was considered a mental illness in the *Diagnostic and Statistical Manual*, the text that psychologists and psychiatrists use to diagnose mental health symptoms. So-called conversion therapy providers have long used the medicalization of gay, lesbian, bisexual, and transgender people as justification for a practice that is known to cause harm. Conversion therapy—a dangerous unscientific practice that attempts to change someone's sexuality, gender, or gender expression—remains legal in nineteen states today, with only 47% of LGBTQ youth living in states that ban conversion therapy for minors.

There is a long history in the US of criminalizing queer and trans people. Laws against crossdressing and any other deviance from strict gender norms began as early as the 1690s in the Massachusetts colony. US cities later followed suit and passed similar ordinances, into the twentieth century. The thirteen original colonies all had sodomy laws that continued for over two hundred years. It wasn't until 2003 that it finally became legal to be gay in all states and territories. That's right—it was still technically illegal in some states to be openly gay until the early 2000s, when the Lawrence v. Texas decision decriminalized homosexuality. This is one of the many reasons why current attacks on LGBTQIA+ people that target gender expression in public (like drag shows) or the teaching of LGBTQIA+ history in schools is extremely alarming to all of us who remember a time when it was quite literally illegal to be out. Globally, there are still sixty-four countries where homosexuality is criminalized.

Even before the riots of the 1950s and '60s and the start of Pride, people would gather in their homes to form organizations. They often couldn't be openly gay, in fear of violence or discrimination, so they organized private groups with thoughtful confidentiality procedures. Quietly yet

BOOKS ABOUT HIV/AIDS ACTIVISM

LET THE RECORD SHOW: A Political History of ACT UP New York, 1987–1993 | Sarah Schulman, Farrar, Straus and Giroux, 2021.

LOVE YOUR ASIAN BODY: AIDS Activism in Los Angeles | Eric C. Wat, University of Washington Press, 2022.

WHEN WE RISE: My Life in the Movement | Cleve Jones, Hachette Books, 2016.

effectively they came together to create groups like the Society for Human Rights, the earliest gay rights organization, founded in Chicago in 1924 by Henry Gerber. Other early organizations included the Mattachine Society (1950) and the Daughters of Bilitis (1955). The Daughters of Bilitis hosted consciousness-raising groups, a term that came from the second-wave feminist and gay liberation movements where people would talk openly for the first time about their sexuality or about experiencing misogyny alongside others going through similar struggles.

Christopher Street Liberation Day March was the very first Pride march, organized by Gay Liberation Front; it took place in 1970 in New York in honor of the Stonewall Inn riots that had broken out in the same location the year before. Pride celebrations have since emerged across the country and around the globe, primarily for Pride Month. The month of June has been officially recognized as a commemorative month in honor of the Stonewall riots: in 1999 by President Bill Clinton as "Gay and Lesbian Pride Month"; in 2009 by President Barack Obama as "LGBT Pride Month"; and in 2021 by President Joe Biden as "LGBTQ Pride Month."

More and more, people took to the streets. The first national march—the National March on Washington for Lesbian and Gay Rights—took place in 1979, with another following fourteen years later in 1993: the March on Washington for Lesbian, Gay, and Bi Equal Rights and Liberation. In more recent history, the first Trans March for Visibility took place in Washington, DC, in 2019 and continues annually.

The Black Lives Matter movement, founded in 2013 by three Black women (two of whom are queer), Alicia Garza, Patrisse Cullors, and Opal Tometi, has organized countless marches across the country for Black lives with an intersectional approach that acknowledges the overlaps in gendered and racialized violence. Throughout this book, you'll read about other marches and school walkouts like the Brooklyn Liberation March, Walkout to Learn, and the March for Queer and Trans Youth Autonomy.

YOUTH TO THE FRONT

Prior to Stonewall, youth groups organized to center the needs of gay and trans youth, including Vanguard (1966); the Homophile Youth Movement in Neighborhoods (1968), which published a periodical; and the Student Homophile League at Columbia University (more on this in chapter 3). Then, in 1969, the group Gay Youth New York, which later became Gay and Lesbian Youth of New York (GLYNY), began its work of combatting the oppression of gay youth. Their slogan, "Youth Organized, Youth Run," created a model for many youth-led and youth-centered organizations to come, like the Boston Alliance of Gay, Lesbian, Bisexual, and Transgender Youth (BAGLY), formed in 1980 in Massachusetts.

INTERSECTIONALITY

Intersectionality is a term that was coined in 1989 by Kimberlé Crenshaw, a legal scholar, to describe the unique experiences of Black women who face overlapping systems of oppression—both racism and sexism. Much like the political analysis made by the **Combahee River Collective** in 1977, Crenshaw's work highlights Black feminist thought and activism.

"NOBODY'S FREE UNTIL EVERYBODY'S FREE."
—FANNIE LOU HAMER, CIVIL RIGHTS ACTIVIST

WHAT WE'RE WORKING TOWARD

Unfortunately, many of the issues that Sylvia Rivera and Marsha P. Johnson worked to eradicate are still present today. The work of achieving LGBTQIA+ liberation will not be done until Black trans people are truly safe and free.

Marginalized people experience not only barriers to accessing resources but also threats to our physical, emotional, and mental safety. LGBTQIA+ youth in particular face disparities in housing and education, and in receiving support for substance use, mental health, bullying, violence, and more. So many queer and trans young people are unhoused. According to a study from the University of Chicago, LGBTQIA+ youth are twice as likely to be unhoused in the United States.

Recent legislation across the US has targeted LGBTQIA+ people's access to gender-affirming care, athletics, education, identification documents, free speech, public spaces, and more. More than 500 anti-LGBTQ bills were proposed in the 2024 state legislative session as of June 2024. For older generations, these bills are familiar remnants of harmful policies of the past that the community has worked tirelessly to change.

The same voices who have made it possible to advance rights for the wider LGBTQIA+ community continue to be marginalized and denied access to basic resources. While there are certainly measures of progress to celebrate and appreciate, it is the unfortunate reality that hate crimes against LGBTQIA+ people are the highest they've been in a decade in the US, with rates of transphobic hate crimes increasing by a staggering 32.9% in 2022. Transgender and gender nonconforming people, mostly transgender women of color, are disproportionately murdered each year as a result of anti-trans and anti-Black violence.

Each year, on the annual observance of Transgender Day of Remembrance on November 20, we mourn and honor those lives taken by anti-trans violence. This special day of community gathering and healing began in 1999, in honor of Rita Hester, a Black trans woman from Allston, Massachusetts, who was murdered in 1998. Gathering to grieve and celebrate the lives of people in our community is one way we protest.

Queer and trans people have always faced criminalization and violence, which has erased much of our history from mainstream ways of

CIVIL RIGHTS ORGANIZING

There is significant overlap between all movements for social justice, and part of thoughtful community organizing is practicing uplifting and giving credit to the organizers who got us here. Civil rights organizers like **Bayard Rustin, Kiyoshi Kuromiya, Angela Davis, James Baldwin**, and many others are activists at the intersections of racial, gender, sexual, and economic justice. In 1970, **Huey Newton**, cofounder of the **Black Panther Party**, delivered a speech acknowledging the overlaps in the Black Power movement with the women's and gay liberation movements. Organizing strategies like sit-ins were pioneered by Black civil rights activists and are effective organizing tools that LGBTQIA+ activists use to this day.

learning and sharing history. There are so many community leaders and activists whose names we will never know. This is why many of us feel so passionately about telling our stories and including LGBTQIA+ contributions in educational spaces. The young people in this chapter envision their work as building upon the many generations of grassroots struggle—and aim to uplift their trancestors (a term coined by CeCe McDonald) through their own work, in hopes that more of us will survive and thrive.

In order to grow movements and make equity a reality, collaboration and coalition building is essential. Building relationships often means we start with understanding ourselves first. The community organizers here have explored, and continue to explore, their own histories, their connection with their biological and chosen families, and their cultures. In developing their own identity, they've reached out for support and found people with shared experiences. This outreach has led to building their own confidence as leaders—and later, creating nonprofits, organizing Pride celebrations, or testifying on their experiences to legislators. Each person attributes their success to the strength of their community, rather than emphasizing their individual achievement.

What is your theory of change? How do you think change is made for queer and trans people? Who are the most effective LGBTQIA+ organizers that you know of? What are our biggest priorities moving forward?

LGBTQIA+ People in the Courts and Government

1866:   Frances Thompson is believed to be the first
transgender person to testify to Congress.

1953:   President Dwight D. Eisenhower bans "homosexuals" from
working in the federal government, leading to the firing of five
thousand people. This is referred to as the Lavender Scare.

1972:   Title IX becomes federal law and prohibits discrimination
on the basis of sex in education and federal financial
assistance. In 2021, the US Department of Education
confirms that Title IX protects students from discrimination
based on sexual orientation and gender identity.

1990:   The Americans with Disabilities Act (ADA) passes, prohibiting
discrimination based on disability. This is a major success for
disability justice advocates. It also impacts people living with HIV/
AIDS, as it adds protection from discrimination in employment,
public accommodations, and other areas during a time when
stigma toward people living with HIV is extremely prevalent.

1992:   The Massachusetts Governor's Commission on Gay and
Lesbian Youth is created, becoming the first independent state
agency dedicated to serving LGBTQIA+ youth. Now called
the Massachusetts Commission on LGBTQ Youth, it continues
to be the first and only in the country and provides LGBTQ-
specific recommendations to Massachusetts state agencies.
In 1993, the MA Safe Schools Program for LGBTQ Students is
founded, also becoming the first in the country to be sponsored

by a Department of Elementary and Secondary Education. Today, it provides free training and customized support to schools and hosts a GSA Student Leadership Council.

1994: The Clinton administration institutes "Don't Ask, Don't Tell," which extends a long-standing ban on openly gay, lesbian, and bisexual people from military service, implying that they can serve only while closeted. It is repealed in 2011, yet the ban on trans people serving openly isn't lifted until 2016.

2009: The Matthew Shepard and James Byrd Jr. Hate Crimes Prevention Act is signed into federal law, expanding protections for victims of crimes motivated by homophobia, transphobia, and ableism.

2015: The US Supreme Court legalizes same-gender marriages in all fifty states in the Obergefell v. Hodges decision.

2016: The US Departments of Justice and Education declare that schools receiving federal money must respect a student's gender identity, including their choice of bathroom. This law is revoked in 2017 by the Trump administration. From 2016 forward, ballot questions and legal battles pop up across the country in Virginia, Alaska, Massachusetts, and other states about trans rights in public accommodations and bathrooms. The Biden administration reaffirms this right in 2021. Read more about how L Austin-Spooner, Katherine Ferreira O'Connor, Gavin Grimm, and Lillian Lennon work to protect public accommodations in this chapter.

2016: Thanks to advocacy by interACT, the US Department of Health and Human Services adds language to the Affordable Care Act's prohibition of sex discrimination in federally funded health programs to clarify that discrimination on the basis of intersex traits is discrimination on the basis of sex. This is the first time the US government explicitly acknowledges legal protections for intersex people.

2017: Andrea Jenkins becomes the first Black openly trans woman to be elected to office in the United States, representing Ward 8 in south central Minneapolis on the City Council. Jenkins is now the president of the city council, and is also a poet, artist, and oral historian who documented the lives of transgender and gender nonconforming people for the Transgender Oral History Project.

2020: In the Bostock v. Clayton County decision, the US Supreme Court confirms that Title VII of the Civil Rights Act of 1964 protects gay and transgender employees against discrimination.

2021: Stella Keating becomes the first transgender teenager to testify before the Senate when she speaks in support of the Equality Act, which would provide federal protections for LGBTQ people in education, employment, health care, housing, and other areas. It has yet to pass.

2021: Jerome Foster, an openly bisexual climate activist, becomes the youngest White House advisor in US history. As a member of the White House Environmental Justice Advisory Council, Jerome was selected to provide recommendations on climate injustice. Formerly, he'd served as an intern for US Representative John Lewis. During this internship, he hosted weekly climate rallies at the White House front gates in collaboration with Greta Thunberg's Fridays for Future movement, which advocated for the passage of the Climate Change Education Act—an act that would add environmental education as a core subject to American schools.

2023: By the end of the year, the ACLU tracked 510 anti-LGBTQIA+ federal and state bills, ranging from restrictions on gender-affirming care to athletics access, from inclusive curriculum and education to freedom of expression by drag performers, and more.

At the height of the AIDS epidemic in the 1980s, when government officials ignored the needs of the gay and trans communities, an intergenerational movement of organizers came together through groups like the AIDS Coalition to Unleash Power (ACT UP), founded in New York City, to stage direct political actions, including die-in protests, where organizers lay in front of governmental institutions and held gravestone signs representing the lives lost to HIV/AIDS due to government inaction to this deadly disease. Across the country in San Francisco, Cleve Jones developed the AIDS Memorial Quilt, a large-scale display of quilt panels to honor thousands of lives. It was first displayed in 1987 during the National March on Washington for Lesbian and Gay Rights, with 1,920 panels; each name was read aloud.

"The community in which I grew up was my biggest
support system. Each person never made me feel
insecure about who I was, and never
made me question myself."
—Andraya Yearwood

ANDRAYA YEARWOOD
(SHE/HER)

Andraya Yearwood is an activist, athlete, and Black transgender woman who envisions a future where everyone can be accepted and embraced for who they are. Running track in high school built her self-confidence and determination, which she carries into the advocacy work she does today.

Andraya is most proud of recently being featured in the Emmy-nominated film *Changing the Game* (2019), a Hulu documentary highlighting the stories of trans high school athletes. Alongside her teammate Terry Miller, the film also features Sarah Rose Huckman, a skier from New Hampshire, and Mack Beggs, a wrestler from Texas. Each young person shares their story of advocating for their right to simply be their full self while competing in the sports they love.

As an athlete at Cromwell High School in Connecticut, Andraya won several state championships and found the most joy in running the 100-meter dash. Unfortunately, she also experienced harassment while competing. In her senior year, a lawsuit criticizing Connecticut's trans-inclusive sports policy was filed against the Connecticut Interscholastic Athletic Conference, multiple school boards, and Andraya and her teammate Terry Miller, attempting to remove the right of transgender athletes to play on a team aligning with their gender identity. The suit was later dismissed by a federal judge, who ruled that discriminating against transgender athletes would violate Title IX. Andraya says that her incredibly supportive family and school community stuck by her throughout high school and in these challenging moments.

During her transition in high school, she recalls, "The administration at the school came up with the idea to have a meeting prior to the start of the school year. In this meeting, I was accompanied by my parents, coaches, nurses, teachers, even my guidance counselor. During the meeting, I remember feeling such a sense of security and genuine care. Everyone in the room made it clear that their arms were wide open. I could tell that my teachers were willing to address me by my preferred name and pronouns, and that my coaches wouldn't make me feel excluded from my teammates. These acts of inclusivity and support continued to be shown all throughout the rest of my time in high school. I could not have asked for a better group of friends or family to stick by my side through the entirety of my transition."

Changing the Game allowed Andraya to connect more deeply with other trans athletes, and she says it expanded her activism to new networks and opportunities across the country. She was chosen for *Teen Vogue*'s 21 Under 21 list in 2020, and in 2022, she was featured in a documentary series called *Running While Black*, created by *Vice* in partnership with Adidas. As a college student at North Carolina Central University, she double majored in Spanish and Race, Gender, and Class Studies, served on the leadership of student government, and studied abroad in Buenos Aires in 2022.

NOTABLE TRANS ATHLETES

CECÉ TELFER: track and field, first openly transgender person to win NCAA title

CHRIS MOSIER: triathlete, first transgender athlete to represent US in international competition, founder of transathlete.com

JAIYAH SAELUA: soccer, first openly nonbinary and trans woman to compete in FIFA World Cup qualifier

JAY PULITANO: swimming, first openly trans man to play on any men's team in the NCAA

KEELIN GODSEY: hammer-throw, first openly transgender athlete to compete for a spot on the United States Olympic team

KYE ALLUMS: basketball, first openly transgender NCAA athlete to play Division I sports

LAYSHIA CLARENDON: basketball, first openly nonbinary WNBA player

LAUREL HUBBARD: weightlifter, first openly trans woman Olympian

LIA THOMAS: swimmer, first openly transgender athlete to win an NCAA Division I championship title

PATRICIO MANUEL: boxer, first openly transgender boxer to fight professionally in the US

SCHUYLER BAILAR: swimmer, first openly transgender NCAA Division I men's athlete in any sport (see chapter 3)

"I hope, after my generation, we get to see the queer youth of the future, the ones to live freely in the most radical sense, being able to express themselves however they see fit, and that institutions will value them instead of challenge or exclude them." —Cyn Macias-Gómez

CYN MACIAS-GÓMEZ
(THEY/HE)

Cyn Macias-Gómez is an advocate and community organizer focused on mental health education and LGBTQIA+ rights. Cyn is passionate about bridging the gap between the many communities they're part of as a queer, Chicano, disabled, Catholic, first-generation student, and says they do everything "in the hopes that I can make it easier for the communities that I come from."

In high school, Cyn took on leadership roles in his GSA and the National Alliance on Mental Illness (NAMI) group. The intersection of these two passions allowed Cyn to focus on mental health as a core component of queer wellness. They say, "Mental health is just not at the forefront of conversations pretty much *ever*, so I think that that's kind of where my work started. It was in that very, you know, selfish way in that I was just looking for community." The skills that Cyn built while finding community soon led them to leadership roles as a member of Mental Health America's Youth Leadership Council, an ambassador for the Tangible Movement (a mental health education organization), and a homelessness commissioner for the City of Berkeley, California. In 2021, Cyn was named to GLAAD's second annual 20 Under 20 list.

Cyn says they are most proud of their work through the UC Washington Program (UCDC) at University of California, Berkeley, a program that sends students to Washington, DC, to have a full experience of public service through internships and classes. At the University of California's Office of the President, Cyn is advocating for undocumented students, and says he's been able to "speak with representatives' offices and really advocate for student needs. It's also given me the institutional knowledge, which is the reason why I go into every space that I do, in hopes that I can not only gain the resources but gain them in a way where I can apply them and give them to other people, because I know that's a huge barrier." Ultimately, Cyn is working toward removing barriers through policy and education so more young people can access the future they deserve.

They say, "We're the ones that are eager to be in these spaces and have a seat at the table, because now we understand how intimidating that is to other people to see that we have the knowledge so early. We're the ones that want to not only ensure that our perspectives, our lives, and our experiences are valued and centered in conversations. We're also the ones wanting to continuously build on the tactics of and methods of change that came before us. We demand that future generations don't have to fight so hard."

When envisioning their future, Cyn plans to become a social worker and a lawyer, run for office, and teach history. They say about law school, "I really want to not only go to law school and become a lawyer for me, but for the amount of resources and knowledge that I can give back. I think that law is one of the most inaccessible fields to go into, so to be able to do it and give it back and have mentorship programs . . . I want to share that I am a queer brown person with all these things happening, but I did it, and you can too and I'm here to help you and make sure that you do. I want to play a crucial role in the future when it comes to organizing for Chicano youth rights and organizing for student rights in general, or people of color, or disability rights, and our rights as a community and our individual axes of oppression that we're experiencing."

SELF-CARE AND COMMUNITY CARE

Organizing can lead us to so many positive connections and experiences. It might teach us more about ourselves and help us celebrate our strengths and values. It can also be stressful and draining at times, so it's important to make time for self-care and community care. Self-care includes the things we do for ourselves to sustain our mental well-being, and community care is how we get support from the people around us.

SELF-CARE	COMMUNITY CARE
Spend time with chosen family and loved ones who support you.	Cook a meal with friends or neighbors.
Know your limits and ask for help! You are one person and you do not have to do everything on your own.	Attend a support group or social gathering related to shared identities or experiences.
Explore your hobbies and interests regularly.	Engage with local mutual aid networks, including asking for support for yourself and sharing your time, resources, or money when you're able to.
Do things that feel good for your body, whether that's exercising, eating nourishing food, or seeking out affirming health care.	Ask friends to give you reminders for important things you need to do.

SELF-CARE	COMMUNITY CARE
Stay connected with parts of your identity, culture, family history, language, and spirituality that are important to you.	Share resources that you've accessed and enjoyed.
Learn about things that interest you just for fun, not for the sake of productivity or achievement.	Volunteer with a local organization.
Listen to your body and respect when you need breaks.	Learn about movements for social justice and how you can support them.

Similarly, as an educator, they hope to mobilize students by sharing knowledge of community history and making sure that "what every generation before us has gone through isn't forgotten."

Cyn's work on mental health has helped them build their own strategies to deal with burnout and stress too. He says that building in consistent times for self-care has been helpful, and is focused on three things: reading, museums, and running. Their recent passion readings are *Women, Race & Class* by Angela Y. Davis and *Continuum* by Chella Man. Museums allow Cyn to feel connected to humanity and history, while running is a soothing physical reset. Cyn says, "It brings me joy that I'm putting myself first in this way where I'm not trying to burn through the work but instead stopping, checking in with myself, finding out that this is something that I need, and going and doing it."

"Activism is speaking for yourself. I never knew how to advocate for myself growing up. I learned that everyone has a different way of expressing themselves. You could protest, start a website, write a story—just put your message out there." —Dehkontee Chanchan

DEHKONTEE CHANCHAN
(SHE/HER & THEY/THEM)

Dehkontee Chanchan is a passionate advocate for housing justice and youth leadership. Dehkontee was born in Monrovia, Liberia, and moved to the United States at nine years old. Their first challenge of advocacy stemmed from growing up in an abusive household, where their dreams of traveling began. While Dehkontee moved between family members and the foster care system, it was hard to focus on school. At sixteen, she was arrested for truancy, which led to opportunities that she says changed her life. With the support of the Department of Youth Rehabilitation Services (DYRS), Dehkontee was able to graduate high school and begin sharing their story with other young people. At DYRS, they spoke on panels and became involved with the youth counselor program. In search of more resources, Dehkontee got connected with several organizations that supported personal growth and housing security.

"Throughout my life, I never had a stable place to stay," Dehkontee recounts. "I finally have a place of my own and I'm in school. I'm most proud of where I'm at right now, especially when I look back at where I started from." Dehkontee's story shares similarities with those of the 4.2 million youth who experience homelessness every year in the United States.

Today, Dehkontee protects those experiencing homelessness. Their professional journey as an advocate for unhoused people first began with HER Resiliency Center, a nonprofit supporting young women, and more recently continued with Miriam's Kitchen. At HER, Dehkontee learned how she could impact others with her story and advocacy skills. As a staff member at HER, Dehkontee accompanied young women experiencing homelessness to doctor and therapist appointments and financial meetings, and helped them access any other resources they needed. "I don't just do it for the women I work with," Dehkontee explains. "I do it for every homeless person living on the street that gets looked over. I bring positivity wherever I can, because I know it's hard to find that when you're homeless."

Dehkontee's committed work was recognized in 2018 when she received the Fabiola & Orlando Letelier Youth Activism Award and was selected as a True Colors United Fellow. At True Colors, Dehkontee met people for the first time who identified as nonbinary and used they/them pronouns. "I was still coming out as lesbian and getting more comfortable," they shared. "Then I became a Fellow at True Colors, and it opened my eyes to even more possibilities." As a Fellow, Dehkontee participated in a research team that got other young people involved in advocating for safe and secure housing for all.

Dehkontee graduated from college with a degree in mental health and has many dreams to explore—whether it's starting her own business or pursuing a social work career. Above all, they see the next chapter of their life focused on travel and adventure. Dehkontee finds joy in spending time with her godchildren, learning Spanish, and dancing. If they could travel to a new place once a month, they would. What are Dehkontee's dreams for her community and the world? They'd like to see affordable housing in DC and more emphasis on youth voices in advocacy work. Dehkontee feels strongly that "youth are the best people to explain their own experiences."

"Young people shape the way we interact with activism. In each generation, organizing is radicalized again and again toward the new world young people anticipate. They show us the way forward."
—Gavin Grimm

GAVIN GRIMM
(HE/HiM)

Gavin Grimm showed up as his full self to high school in rural Virginia, and with the support of his mom, he talked with the school administrators about the supports he needed to be respected at school as a transgender boy. For nearly two months, his school respected his name, pronouns, and need to access the boys' restroom. Yet the complaints of parents and residents in his school's county persuaded the school board to prevent Gavin from using the boys' restroom. When he graduated in 2017, the school also refused to print "male" on his transcript. Gavin's self-advocacy soon made him the voice of a major court case, Grimm v. Gloucester County School Board. Gavin and his lawyers from the American Civil Liberties Union

FOURTEENTH AMENDMENT

The Fourteenth Amendment's Equal Protection Clause was written to provide everyone with "equal protection of the laws." Specifically, the Constitution was ratified in 1868, after the Civil War, to prevent discrimination against Black people. It is a relevant clause that judges might consider in cases involving someone's identity, especially protected categories like race, socioeconomic status, gender, or national origin. The Supreme Court has yet to decide if sexual orientation is protected under the Equal Protection Clause, though this certainly came into question in 2015 during the *Obergefell v. Hodges* decision, which ultimately allowed for same-sex marriage across the country.

(ACLU) argued that his rights had been violated under Title IX and the Fourteenth Amendment's Equal Protection Clause.

In 2017, Gavin's case was scheduled to go before the Supreme Court. It would have been the first case that the Supreme Court heard regarding transgender rights. However, the Trump administration rescinded Obama-era guidance advocating for the rights of transgender students, and the case was sent to the lower courts. His story was featured in *Gender Revolution: A Journey with Katie Couric*, which first aired on National Geographic in 2017. At the time, Gavin was preparing for the Supreme Court to hear his case and shared, "This could go really well or it could go really wrong, and I have to be prepared for that reality. But regardless of what happens, the ends will justify the means, because even if we suffer a loss, we've generated a conversation that moves the nation in the right direction." It's true—Gavin's story did influence conversations around the country about transgender students' rights in schools, and it inspired other youth to advocate for their rights at school.

After Gavin had spent more than six and a half years fighting for his rights, the US District Court for the Eastern District of Virginia ruled that Gavin's school had violated his rights under Title IX and the Fourteenth Amendment. When Gavin got the news that his case had been won, he was in the San Francisco Bay area, where he was taking college courses at the time, with plans to become a middle school English teacher. When asked what he's most proud of, Gavin says, "As far as I know, the reward has just been the privilege of being in the community itself. I'm so, so proud of my trans identity specifically, and seeing it as such an important and beautiful part of myself to be celebrated. It is something that enhances my quality of life and enhances who I am and my experiences."

Today Gavin is also a nationally renowned speaker and visits schools across the country to share his story. His first book, *If You're a Kid Like Gavin*, written with Kyle Lukoff and illustrated by J Yang, tells the story of how Gavin advocated for himself—and how all young people have the power to do the same.

For fun, Gavin loves taking walks with his mischievous cat, Rascal, and is a longtime Pokémon fan. He hopes to become a foster parent at some point, and to create a physical space for LGBTQ people. "It would be supercool if I could open up some kind of LGBTQ community center around the community that I grew up in, in Virginia, where there were just no resources. We drove two hours to the closest support group in Richmond, Virginia, so that's a dream of mine."

"My politics are personal because I am one of few
who lives to tell my story; my advocacy is my means
to strengthen the courage of those I love."
—Kaylyn Ahn

KAYLYN AHN
(SHE/THEY)

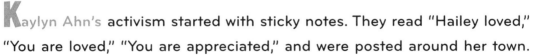

Kaylyn Ahn's activism started with sticky notes. They read "Hailey loved," "You are loved," "You are appreciated," and were posted around her town. After Kaylyn's best friend, Hailey Muro, died by suicide in May 2019, Kaylyn says they "realized the impact that I could have on my own healing and the healing of my community." Kaylyn and Hailey had shared so much joy together, including celebrating their queerness. After founding the Hailey Loved Project, Kaylyn's activism expanded and soon led to organizing protests and eventually passing legislation in her state of Illinois.

As a Korean American daughter of immigrants, Kaylyn has been vocal about the impact of racism on their own life and on the lives of students in her community. In late 2020, Kaylyn created a petition with the D214 Justice Group, a coalition of students and teachers advocating for racial equity and school disciplinary reform, calling on their school district to end the ways they were perpetuating systemic racism, especially for BIPOC students impacted by the COVID-19 pandemic. District 214 students of color were suspended and expelled at higher rates than white students, which is a widespread, unfair trend in districts across the country. The D214 Justice Group asked for restorative justice reforms, anti-racist curricula, and a diversity, equity, and inclusion (DEI) director.

Several months later, Kaylyn organized the March for Asian Lives in Arlington Heights, Illinois, to honor the eight lives lost to anti-Asian violence in Atlanta in a spa in March 2021. More than a march, it was a way for people participating to support local Asian-owned businesses along

the route. This included Kaylyn's aunt's Korean grocery store, Bada Foods, which would eventually shut down due to pandemic restrictions. As a local small business, it struggled to compete with the larger, corporate Asian grocery stores. Protesters were encouraged to stop and shop at small businesses, amplifying the importance of pairing words with action. For Pride Month, Kaylyn also organized Say It With Pride: Equality Now!, a protest that successfully pushed for the repealment, in several towns, of ordinances that banned people from dressing in clothing that didn't align with their sex assigned at birth.

In June 2022, Kaylyn experienced "one of the most powerful moments of [their] life" when they spoke at a bill signing for HB5441, legislation that added protections for survivors of sexual assault in Illinois. Kaylyn became a survivor in 2021 and unfortunately experienced injustice and victim-blaming when they reported the assault to the police. After the police department refused to press charges against her rapist, Kaylyn wrote to their local representative to draft the bill, which amended the Illinois statute of consent and created greater protections for survivors who are assaulted while using substances. Previously under Illinois statute, a lack of consent was only considered when a victim was given the intoxicating substance by the perpetrator. If the substance was taken voluntarily, the attack while under the influence did not qualify as assault. Kaylyn argued that "it doesn't matter whether the perpetrator gave you the substance, or you took it yourself voluntarily. It's assault." She testified in front of the Illinois Senate and House, where the bill passed unanimously. With Kaylyn standing alongside Governor J. B. Pritzker, the bill was signed into law on June 16, 2022. Kaylyn says, "It felt like I was taking back my autonomy and I felt like I was taking back my voice, and that people were listening to me for the first time." Now, police departments across the state are mandated to train their officers about the law's proper enforcement. It's rendered over 7,000 previously unaddressed sexual assault cases eligible for prosecution and increases by thousands each year.

From sticky notes to petitions to protests to state legislation, Kaylyn has been actively engaged in her community and advocating for a better future for all young people. In 2021 their work was acknowledged by GLAAD's 20 Under 20 list, which highlights young LGBTQ leaders shaping the future of media and activism. Looking ahead, Kaylyn dreams of a career in public service. She wants to "provide resources to people in times of need, because when I was assaulted, I didn't have that." In pursuit of this career, she has interned at the US Special Envoy for Afghan Women, Girls, and Human Rights, the White House Initiative on Asian Americans, Native Hawaiians, and Pacific Islanders, and the US Embassy in South Africa. In 2024, she was named a Truman Scholar for Illinois, receiving the premier graduate scholarship for aspiring public service leaders in the US.

Kaylyn finds joy in reading, art, and performing slam poetry. Their favorite book is *This Bridge Called My Back*, a collection of writings by radical women of color, edited by Cherríe Moraga and Gloria Anzaldúa. Hailey, Kaylyn's beloved friend, loved writing poetry too, and had plans to publish her work. In 2022, Kaylyn actualized that dream and published *Grades and other poems (my perspective on the world and myself)* by Hailey Muro, and is donating all profits to queer organizations.

"In the past, very few people had access.
Now it's the lucky few who have access."
—L Austin-Spooner

"Our role is to push justice forward while keeping
our shared histories and ancestors close and
our collective radical imagination active."
—Katherine Ferreira O'Connor

L AUSTIN-SPOONER
(THEY/HE)
&
KATHERINE FERREIRA O'CONNOR
(THEY/THEM)

 Austin-Spooner and Katherine Ferreira O'Connor came together with a common purpose: protecting trans rights. They first met in 2018 when Massachusetts introduced a ballot question that would repeal protections for trans people in places of public accommodation. The campaign they teamed up on was called Yes on 3, a grassroots effort to educate the public and make sure trans rights weren't overturned. They worked alongside other youth, including Ashton Mota (featured in chapter 3).

"We wanted to train other activists, so we hosted trainings for phone banks, door-to-door campaigning, and testimony writing. Youth went to the state house to present what we created at the testimony-writing workshop," L said. Both L and Katherine felt it was important that advocacy for issues directly impacting youth was led by youth themselves, and they were proud

PUBLIC ACCOMMODATIONS
Both Lillian Lennon and Gavin Grimm, who are both featured in this chapter, have advocated for public accommodations in other states and fought against harmful restrictions on trans people's access to public spaces too.

ADULTISM IN ORGANIZING SPACES

Adultism is a system of oppression that affords adults more power than youth. For instance, voting begins at eighteen even though political decisions impact all young people's lives. There are efforts across the country to lower the voting age to give more young people a say in their democracy. Adultism shows up in organizing spaces too. Katherine says they received comments like "I'm glad your generation is fixing things," or "Who's in charge?" when they were very clearly in charge. These comments unfairly imply that young people are responsible for finding solutions to society's problems, and yet when they are, their leadership is questioned or minimized.

that Yes on 3 in particular was "a trans and nonbinary youth-led effort." They also worked to improve language accessibility by providing all materials in Spanish and Portuguese in partnership with Massachusetts Jobs with Justice, a coalition of community, faith, and labor groups focused on labor rights in Massachusetts.

L, a mixed Caribbean American transmasculine person, had just come out as trans about a year before their first Yes on 3 meeting. He says, "I was so inspired by the connection in that space and it made me want to come back. It was a no-judgment space. I felt pushed to do new, scary things." Katherine, a Boston native and mixed Brazilian, says that "seeing visibly nonbinary and gender nonconforming people in the space made me want to advocate for my pronouns more. When you see trans people who look like you in leadership, it really makes a difference."

When L and Katherine faced adultism and tokenism in their work, they kept reminding themselves that their experiences were valuable and just as meaningful as adults'. Their connections with queer youth and adults of color doing similar advocacy work also helps keep them grounded and connected to advocacy work. L says, "I continue to look up to all of the trans adults of color in my life who help me to embrace my Transness and my Blackness every day."

In 2019, Katherine and L accepted the Advancing Equity Award from the Massachusetts Commission on LGBTQ Youth for their successful leadership of the campaign.

After Yes on 3 passed, Katherine and L say, "We got bored. We went to a local ice cream shop to write thank-you notes while we waited for the next campaign." Soon enough, they had three more projects to organize on, including banning conversion therapy and adding the option of X gender markers on state licenses, both of which were successful efforts in Massachusetts.

Katherine and L have so many freedom dreams for LGBTQIA+ communities, including the much-needed abolition of the prison and medical industrial complex, decriminalizing sex work, the devotion of more resources to trans elders and trans youth of color, greater incorporation of disability justice frameworks in the queer movement, the advancement of more BIPOC trans people to leadership roles, building out economic and housing justice, and seeing their trans friends grow into adulthood.

L and Katherine both find so much meaning in celebrating trans joy, for themselves and all trans people, and see this as foundational to liberation for trans youth. Both Katherine and L are still exploring their focus in this work—whether that's through legislation and political advocacy, grassroots direct service work, training and education, or something else. L has gotten more involved in direct work with trans youth, including work supporting harm reduction, job skills, and leadership development at schools, summer camps, and youth programs. Katherine is involved with liberatory curricula design and research at Northwestern University, with a focus on first-generation and lower-income college experiences, and is interested in fugitive queer design and world-building through emergent strategy.

"First and foremost, I want to be outspoken and active in the community. I'm hoping that through my work, I can help other people make that same leap and advocate for their community. I want to see this movement grow."
—Lillian Lennon

LILLIAN LENNON
(SHE/THEY)

Lillian Lennon grew up in Talkeetna, Alaska, with dreams of becoming a filmmaker. She finished her first semester of college in film, and then advocacy called. "I was eighteen and didn't think of myself as much of an activist. I just had increasingly fewer reasons not to take a stand," Lillian says. They soon became known as an effective field organizer when they hosted the first Pride festival to take place in Talkeetna. Not long after that, Lillian learned more about the fight for transgender rights in her state. An ordinance in Alaska had protected transgender and gender nonconforming people from discrimination in public bathrooms and locker rooms since 2015. In 2017, however, a group of opponents tried to take away that right with a ballot question called Proposition 1, insisting that people should use the bathroom of their assigned sex at birth.

Though Lillian was new to activism when this ballot question emerged, she was no stranger to discrimination. As a transgender woman who was subjected to conversion therapy as a fourteen-year-old, Lillian knows what it's like to experience transphobia from strangers and those closest to you. Lillian has seen prejudice and wants to do something about it.

From August 2017 to the final vote in April 2018, Lillian and other volunteers knocked on doors and called the homes of Anchorage voters. These dedicated volunteers understood that transphobia is, in part, fueled by misconceptions and stigma. They knew that empathy-building and education are necessary to debunk harmful stereotypes. Lillian, as the field organizer for this campaign, organized volunteers and coalitions, assisted with target mapping and messaging, and worked on the front lines, knocking on the doors of people who had, to their knowledge, never met a trans person before. Her job was to share the facts—that trans people deserve equal rights, including safe access to bathrooms and locker rooms, that trans people don't pose a threat to others simply through their existence or by using the bathroom, and that the time for trans liberation is now.

After months of knocking on doors and phone banking, Proposition 1 was defeated and trans rights were upheld in Anchorage, Alaska! Lillian says this is their proudest accomplishment yet, but that the work is far from over. "Alaska and the United States' patchwork system of protections continues to enable anti-trans discrimination and violence." However, Alaska's success sent a message to the rest of the country that trans rights are human rights, and that this community will no longer be marginalized. Lillian understands that a future where trans people thrive isn't just about policy—it's about community.

Alongside organizing Talkeetna Pride each year, she's also busy finding ways to uplift other trans leaders in Alaska. Lillian and trans leaders from the Fair Anchorage campaign created Trans Leadership Alaska, which is nourishing sustainable and proactive trans leadership through policy and community by working with Choosing Our Roots, which houses queer and trans houseless youth. When asked what they do for fun, Lillian laughs and asks, "Can I say my work in advocacy?" But Alaskan summers, illustration, and filmmaking continue to bring Lillian joy too.

"In my activism, the moments when I have felt
the most successful is when I have caused
people to reawaken. And how do you make people
reawaken? It's by making them feel again."
—Sherenté Mishitashin Harris

SHERENTÉ MISHITASHIN HARRIS
(ALL PRONOUNS)

Sherenté Mishitashin Harris is a Two-Spirit artist, cultural educator, and citizen of the Narragansett Indian Tribe. They were named an LGBT History Month Icon in 2019. On joy, they say, "One of my greatest joys is helping others to come to that same mode of living that their ancestors, too, once knew intimately and well. All people at one point lived close to the earth, with respect and reverence for the earth . . . If we can bring people back to that place, my hope is that it will do our world some good."

In 2021, *Being Thunder* was released, a film about Sherenté's life from the ages of fourteen to eighteen and their performances of traditional dance in competitions at regional Powwows. Powwows today are big intertribal events where Indigenous people come together to dance and reconnect. Sherenté wears traditional female dress and dances with authenticity, joy, and admiration for their community's traditions. They come from a family of champion

POWWOWS

The word *Powwow* comes from *Pauwau*, which in the Narragansett language means "Medicine Person," a figure who is central to these ceremonies. The Narragansett tribe is known for holding the oldest recorded Powwow in American history. They have continued to celebrate their "August Meeting" Powwow for more than 347 years.

dancers, including their mother, who toured across the world; their father, a world-champion Eastern war dancer who won at the Schemitzun Powwow; and their grandmother, a world-champion Eastern blanket dancer.

Sherenté says, "Dancing is something that I have been doing since before I was born: in my mother's womb." Yet Sherenté has experienced times when they questioned their future as a dancer. They say, "I faced so much hatred, homophobia, and transphobia. I've had slurs yelled at me growing up. I was bullied. There were times when I didn't feel that it was worth it to continue fancy shawl dancing. But then what turned me around from that was the young people that reached out to me during that dire time, and [who] expressed how valuable everything that I was doing was to them."

Sherenté is most proud of recently being named a leading student in the Rhode Island School of Design (RISD) painting department. They say, "It was an incredible honor, because visual arts was something that for a long time I didn't think I was ever going to be involved in at my high school. We had no art classes, and so I applied to RISD on a whim, and every piece I started making at that time went into my portfolio. I'm so thankful because my artwork has become a new outlet for my activism to work as a vehicle for all of the things that I care about, and when I see all the different things that I do, it's like many spokes on a wheel that all connect back to my people, whether that's my Two-Spirit people or my Narragansett people: that is the center for me."

At RISD, Sherenté also created a land acknowledgment for the university, acknowledging Narragansett people as the traditional stewards of the land. They reached out to student groups on campus to garner support to include more voices, and then released a seven-page statement and a resource guide. This action was about waking people up and honoring Narragansett people. They then called for nearby Brown University, also on Narragansett land, to create an official University Land Acknowledgment to correct errors in unofficial land acknowledgments across campus. Sherenté helped draft Brown's Land Acknowledgment to the Narragansett People, and officially shared it at their 2022 commencement ceremony.

Sherenté says, "Our Two-Spirit people traditionally are the ones in our community that are there to wake everyone up to serve as mediators within the community, because Two-Spirit people serve as the bridge between those things that are seemingly opposite to each other. But the Two-Spirits remind us that really those opposite things are connected in that sacred circle with no beginning and no end. When I say 'wake us,' I mean waking us up out of a programmatic way of thinking."

"Rose B. Simpson, an Indigenous artist, was once told: 'In order to decolonize your mind, you first must feel your heart and you need to break your heart so that you, your heart, can feel again.' People saw me as an idea. They saw me as their adversary, and when they saw me suffering, they saw the pain that I was in. For a moment, they recognized a piece of themselves within me that bridged the gap."
—Sherenté Mishitashin Harris

Sherenté takes great pride and joy in both dancing and writing. They recently finished the draft of a novel titled *The Tradition Keeper*, about their spiritual journey through dance informed by intergenerational trauma, decolonization, and healing. On growth, Sherenté says, "Our people say that in one of our creation stories we are made from the trees, and the trees are a symbol for the universe. Its roots go into the realm that is far below us. Its trunk goes through our realm, and its branches reach up toward the sky world and point to the cardinal directions. All around us. And so, in that way, we're born of the universe and in the same way as the trees, we grow and change just as all life does."

"Trans young people have been spoken for a lot.
So I'm really glad that now, and recently, a lot of
young trans people have spoken up and talked for
themselves and told people how they felt."
—Skyler Morrison

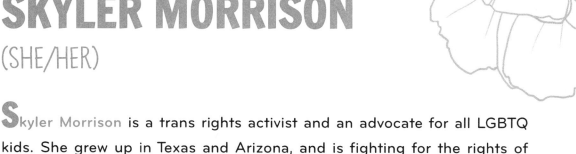

SKYLER MORRISON
(SHE/HER)

Skyler Morrison is a trans rights activist and an advocate for all LGBTQ kids. She grew up in Texas and Arizona, and is fighting for the rights of trans kids in both states. Skyler's caring family decided to move to Phoenix, Arizona, to protect her from harmful anti-trans legislation being proposed and passed in Texas. She feels really lucky to have supportive parents to whom she didn't have to come out. She says, "From a very young age I was able to tell my parents exactly who I was and who I would grow up to be and they listened and believe me. They say I'm the one driving the bus, and they're just in the back seat for support."

Skyler has spoken up for trans kids like her at testimony hearings, rallies, and through online spaces. In 2022, she voiced her opposition to SB1165 in Arizona, which would ban trans youth from participating in the sports team that aligns with their gender identity. She said, "I've had my childhood ripped away by legislators for seven years, and I'm sick of fighting for my human rights, but I won't stop until I know that me and all my transgender friends are safe." She pointed out that legislators are attempting to create a solution to a nonexistent issue, and in doing so, they are harming and discriminating against transgender girls. Since then, Skyler and her family have continued to advocate for trans youth and families, and have partnered with other activists, like her friend Kai Shappley, whose family recently fled Texas to find safety in Connecticut. Other trans girls who came before her, like Jazz Jennings, are an inspiration to Skyler and the activism work she does.

Skyler loves spending time with her friends, especially for trips to the mall, playing video games, swimming, and bike riding. Her next big dream is to be cast in a TV show or movie. She says, "My dream job is to be an actress, and so I'm really trying to work towards that goal, and I'm really hoping that in the future I will become one."

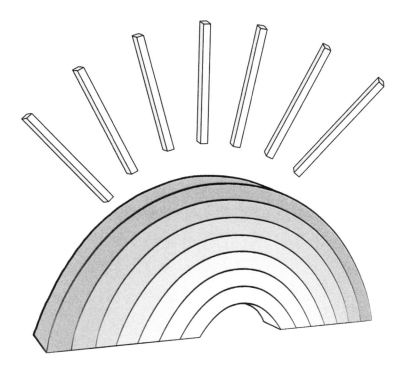

"As legislation targets queer and trans youth more than ever before, it is essential that queer and trans youth are given the opportunity to direct the response."
—Zander Moricz

ZANDER MORICZ
(HE/HIM)

Zander Moricz is a community organizer focused on action projects defending human rights, a "fabulous gay man," and the youngest plaintiff in the "Don't Say Gay" lawsuit in Florida. For all four years of high school at Pine View School in Osprey, Florida, Zander was class president, making him the first openly gay person to serve in this role.

When Florida passed a bill effectively banning discussions of sexual orientation and gender identity in classrooms, Zander co-hosted a rally in Sarasota, led a walkout at his school, and later sued the state for this harmful legislation. He says, "Lawsuits are structured around human beings and their stories because people understand and act through empathy. There are so many queer students who are not in positions where they can safely or comfortably share their identities, so I decided that if I could, I had to—for myself and for those whose stories are being erased."

Zander is the founder and executive director of the Social Equity and Education (SEE) Initiative, which empowers organizers to drive change within their communities and unify their respective efforts into a cohesive, national movement for justice. The organization is focused on direct, in-person actions, like protests and voter registration. They've supported over two thousand new activists, hosted protests in Florida in opposition to the "Don't Say Gay" bills and restrictions on AP African American History classes, and registered thousands of voters. He started the organization during his sophomore year of high school because he says that violent

WALKOUT TO LEARN

On April 21, 2023, Florida high school and college students walked out of their classrooms to learn. Recent legislation proposed and passed by Governor Ron DeSantis and Florida legislators restricted access to books and education, particularly focused on African American history (like AP African American Studies) and gender/queer studies. Zander Moricz and his organization, the Social Equity and Education Alliance, called on all Floridians to organize the largest student protest in Florida's history. While walking out, students learned a piece of history banned by the Florida legislature, signed an active voter pledge, and enrolled in an online African American history course. Rallies took place later that evening in Jacksonville, Miami, Orlando, and Sarasota.

policies from politicians "have created a demand for community support structures that are independent from the government."

His passion for educational equity began with his own firsthand experiences of disparities in education—the difference between well-resourced schools and under-resourced schools. He says, "As I taught, tutored, and volunteered [in under-resourced schools], my bucket couldn't seem to stop any boats from sinking. I could help a class of students, but next session, children with parallel issues would still come through that door. They would continue to come long after I had left, and they had started coming before I was born. I stepped back and reflected on what I was doing and the impact I was trying to have: teachers cannot save both students and the system. So I decided that I would find a way to help teachers help students— holistically helping the system."

Experiencing these disparities inspired Zander to attend school board meetings, where, he says, "The problem was not only structural, but inherently political and intersectional. So I created SEE as a way for my college student body to organize and platform their voice. We uniquely focused on physical activism—the type that much of Gen Z has left behind for digital activism—which brought attention, resources, and momentum to our work. As it turns out, Gen Z has always had the motivation and capacity to bring their advocacy offline; they just haven't had the support to do so. SEE became that support for many—now we're here." Zander's program curates programming specifically to engage marginalized youth and offers safe and affirming spaces to discuss sexual health and identity, which they likely have limited access to due to the pervasive legislation.

He finds so much joy in playing beach volleyball, roller-skating, hunting for campy pieces in thrift stores, practicing yoga, and running an infamous undercover Tripadvisor food critic account. Zander brings together friends and family for "team meetings" to watch shows like *Broad City* and *Abbott Elementary*, order takeout, and help each other live in the moment.

In telling his story publicly and regularly speaking at Sarasota public hearings, he has faced a lot of negative pushback and hate. He says, "I meditate every day to ensure that I am being intentional with how I spend my energy. We have to remember that, first and foremost, activism is self-defense. So if your activism is at the expense of your mental or physical health, you're doing something wrong."

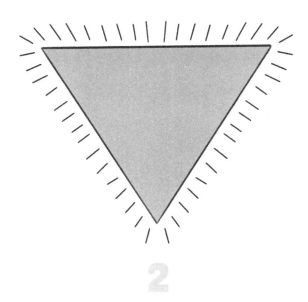

2

ARTISTS

When was the first time you saw yourself reflected in the media, or in any work of art? A moment where you felt your identities, or lived experiences, were recognized through the representation of a character or artist? What was it like to connect with that artist through a screen, book, or performance?

In the words of Marian Wright Edelman, founder of the Children's Defense Fund, "It's hard to be what you can't see." Seeing our stories and experiences portrayed in art can be a powerful opportunity to connect with our inner selves while recognizing there is a broader community we can relate to. Rather than the idea of a role model, which puts people on unrealistic pedestals, a possibility model (a term that Laverne Cox has used to describe herself) shows us that people who share similar identities and experiences can thrive and live full lives.

In 2007, Jazz Jennings was five years old when she shared her experiences as a transgender girl with Barbara Walters on national television, making her one of the youngest people to have come out publicly, then or now. For many of us, Jazz was the first transgender young person we saw in the media. We might have seen a movie or show with a transgender

WHO WE SEE REPRESENTED IN ART SENDS US A MESSAGE ABOUT WHO IS VALUABLE.

character, yet many of these characters weren't played by actual transgender people. Jazz is not an actor—she tells her own story from her perspective. Since then, Jazz has been featured in a television show, *I Am Jazz* (2015–ongoing), and has written a children's book with the same title. In 2016, she became the youngest-ever grand marshal for New York City Pride.

More than fifty years earlier, Christine Jorgensen became the first trans person to become globally famous after receiving gender-affirming surgery. In 1952, the *New York Daily* published an article titled "Ex-GI Becomes Blonde Beauty: Operations Transform Bronx Youth." In 1967, she released an autobiography chronicling her experiences as a trans woman, *Christine Jorgensen: A Personal Autobiography*. Though Jorgensen was publicly sharing her story, many generations of trans people at the time and since have not had this privilege or access. Jazz Jennings's acts of public visibility build on many generations of queer and trans youth leaders before her who could not be as visible for many reasons. *Disclosure*, a documentary film released in 2020, describes the history of trans people on the screen through interviews with modern trans activists, filmmakers, and artists like Laverne Cox, Alexandra Billings, Yance Ford, Tiq Milan, Leo Sheng, Jen Richards, Rain Valdez, and others. It made the underrepresented histories of trans people in media more visible, and chronicles this long history of trans people on screen.

Whether it's on television, in the news, or in daily conversation, LGBTQ+ people have long been erased or silenced

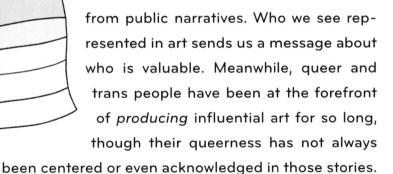

from public narratives. Who we see represented in art sends us a message about who is valuable. Meanwhile, queer and trans people have been at the forefront of *producing* influential art for so long, though their queerness has not always been centered or even acknowledged in those stories. There are so many examples of LGBTQ+ authors, artists, and innovators that we learned about in school, but were never taught explicitly that they were part of the community. Saying that out loud matters. It allows LGBTQ+ people to feel seen in their classrooms, and it also allows everyone else to learn about the contributions of LGBTQ+ people. Think of the Harlem Renaissance (1910s–1930s) with lesbian blues singer Gladys Bentley; the Alvin Ailey American Dance Theater (1950s–present), founded by its namesake, who was a trailblazer of

BALLROOM CULTURE

Ball culture, with roots in the mid-19th century drag balls hosted by William Dorsey Swann, has evolved into a vibrant subculture celebrated for its elaborate competitions and family-like structures known as "houses." By the early 20th century, integrated drag balls gained popularity in major US cities, providing a space for the queer community to express and affirm their identities. Despite early racial biases, figures like Crystal LaBeija catalyzed the creation of contemporary ballroom culture in the 1970s, establishing the first house, the Royal House of LaBeija, in response to discrimination. These houses, offering kinship and support, anchor the culture's competitive events where participants "walk" in various categories, including the iconic dance style, vogue. Ball culture, immortalized in media like **Paris Is Burning**, remains a cornerstone of the Black and Latinx queer community.

modern dance and also a gay man who died of complications related to AIDS in 1989; the disco era of the 1970s with musicians such as Sylvester and Elton John; the ballroom community of New York City (1970s–present), which has been a safe place for LGBTQ+ people to express their artistry and their whole selves; and of course drag performances such as on the main stage of *RuPaul's Drag Race* (2000s–present). In these and so many other spaces and times, queer people have constantly reimagined the intersections of music, movement, and fashion.

You've likely also learned about classic authors who were part of the LGBTQ+ community but maybe had to be private during their lifetime, or whose identity isn't always acknowledged in classrooms—people like Emily Dickinson, Langston Hughes, Walt Whitman, Virginia Woolf, and Alain LeRoy Locke.

Because LGBTQIA+ people have contributed so greatly to the arts, this chapter is structured more like a choose-your-own-adventure. Let your curiosity lead you to listening to a new musician or reading poetry from an artist mentioned here. Can you find out more about who their inspirations were? Who are the LGBTQ+ artists that you admire already, and what is it about their work that inspires you?

The youth artists in this chapter have a brilliant way of portraying the human experience through their many forms of creative expression—whether that's photography, filmmaking, illustration, music, poetry, or social media. They've also found powerful ways to connect arts with activism—artivism! They build on the many legacies of community organizers who understand the power of the arts to advance movements for justice.

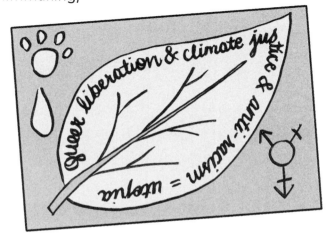

BANNED BOOKS
MOST BANNED BOOKS IN 2022 ACCORDING TO PEN AMERICA.

What do these books have in common?

1. *GENDER QUEER: A Memoir* | Maia Kobabe, Oni Press, 2019 | 41 bans
2. *ALL BOYS AREN'T BLUE* | George M. Johnson, Farrah, Straus and Giroux, 2020 |29 bans
3. *OUT OF DARKNESS* | Ashley Hope Pérez, Carolrhoda Lab, 2015 | 24 bans
4. *THE BLUEST EYE* | Toni Morrison, Holt, Rinehart and Winston, 1970 | 22 bans
5. (tie). *THE HATE U GIVE* | Angie Thomas, Balzer + Bray, 2017 | 17 bans
5. (tie). *LAWN BOY* | Jonathan Evison, Algonquin Books, 2018 | 17 bans

A full list of book recommendations, including children's and young adult recommendations as well as adult nonfiction, is included at the end of this book (see page 213).

(see page 213)

The American Library Association (ala.org/bbooks) and We Need Diverse Books (diversebooks.org) offer resources to help if books are being challenged in your district or community. Banned Books Week (bannedbooksweek.org) is held every September around the world and is a celebration of the right to read.

BOOKS ABOUT LGBTQ ART HISTORY

AND THE CATEGORY IS . . . : Inside New York's Vogue, House, and Ballroom Community | Ricky Tucker, Beacon Press, 2022.

BOWIE MADE ME GAY: 100 Years of LGBT Music | Darryl W. Bullock, Abrams Press, 2017.

GLITTER AND CONCRETE: A Cultural History of Drag in New York City | Elyssa Maxx Goodman, Hanover Square Press, 2023.

QUEER X DESIGN: 50 Years of Signs, Symbols, Banners, Logos, and Graphic Art of LGBTQ | Andy Campbell, Black Dog & Leventhal, 2019.

MUSICIANS

HAYLEY KIYOKO
JANELLE MONÁE
LAURA JANE GRACE
MEET ME @ THE ALTAR
MUNA
OMAR APOLLO
RINA SAWAYAMA
RYAN CASSATA
SAM SMITH
SHEA DIAMOND
SYD
TEGAN AND SARA

JANELLE MONÁE

WRITERS AND POETS

AIDEN THOMAS
AKWAEKE EMEZI
ALICE WALKER
AUDRE LORDE
GEORGE M. JOHNSON
GLORIA ANZALDÚA
JAMES BALDWIN
KACEN CALLENDER
KAY ULANDAY BARRETT
KIT YAN
KYLE LUKOFF
ROXANE GAY

AKWAEKE EMEZI

VISUAL ARTISTS

ASHLEY LUKASHEVSKY
CATHERINE OPIE
FRIDA KAHLO
JEAN-MICHEL BASQUIAT
KEHINDE WILEY
KEITH HARING
MAIA KOBABE
MELANIE GILLMAN
MIA SAINE
MICKALENE THOMAS
NOAH GRIGNI
THEO GRIMES

FRIDA KAHLO

PERFORMANCE

AARON ROSE PHILIP
ASIA KATE DILLON
BILAL BAIG
BOWEN YANG
CHELLA MAN
ELLIOT PAGE
JES TOM
LANA AND LILLY WACHOWSKI
LAVERNE COX
LENA WAITHE
MACDOESIT
NYLE DIMARCO
RAIN VALDEZ

CHELLA MAN

LGBTQ+ People Creating Art and Making History

1958: A landmark Supreme Court decision, One, Inc. v. Olesen, ruled that free speech rights apply to publications focused on homosexuality.

1971: The Stonewall Award is established, the first and most enduring award for LGBTQIA+ books. Recent award recipients include Akwaeke Emezi, Elyssa Maxx Goodman, Lamya H, Malinda Lo, Kyle Lukoff, Sarah Schulman, and Rivers Solomon, among others.

1978: Gilbert Baker is encouraged by Harvey Milk to create a symbol of the community and creates the first Pride flag, with eight colors. By 1979, it had been reduced to the six colors used today, representing life, healing, sunlight, nature, harmony/peace, and spirit. Flags for the community, and all the identities within it, have grown over time. In 1999, Monica F. Helms created the trans flag with pink, blue, and white stripes. In 2017, Amber Hikes and Teri Gerbec in Philadelphia added black and brown stripes, representing BIPOC communities, to the top of the Pride flag. Daniel Quasar created the Progress flag in 2018, incorporating the stripes of all three of these flags in a new design.

1980: Barbara Smith, a founder of the Black feminist Combahee River Collective, creates Kitchen Table: Women of Color Press, which publishes authors like Audre Lorde, Merle Woo, Angela Davis, and other feminist writers.

1986: Joseph Beam, a Black gay rights activist, publishes *In the Life: A Black Gay Anthology*, the first collection of nonfiction writing by Black gay men.

1990:   The documentary film *Paris Is Burning* is released, chronicling ballroom culture in New York City, and introduces a broader audience to legends like Pepper LaBeija, Angie Xtravaganza, Dorian Corey, and Willi Ninja.

2000:   *The Laramie Project*, a production developed by the Tectonic Theater Project, premieres in Denver in February and later transfers to New York City in May. After Matthew Shepard was killed in 1998 at age twenty-one in Laramie, Wyoming, in a violent hate crime, members of the Tectonic Theater Project interviewed residents of Laramie about their reactions to the crime. *The Laramie Project* has become one of the most frequently performed plays in America with its significant impact on cultural understandings of homophobia, especially in schools.

2001:   LGBTQ youth of color found FIERCE! NYC in 2000, a nonprofit built to empower LGBTQ youth with resources to lead in their communities. The following year, they release *Fenced OUT*, a documentary exploring experiences for LGBTQ people of color at the New York piers throughout the 1970s and 1980s.

2006:   Portrayed by Daniel Sea, a trans nonbinary actor, Max Sweeney becomes the first recurring transmasculine character on a television show in *The L Word*.

2017:   Avery Jackson makes history as the first transgender person to be featured on the cover of *National Geographic*, a 128-year-old publication. She is nine years old when this issue of the magazine is released, in January 2017.

SYMBOLS

The LGBTQ+ community has claimed many different symbols over time to signify queerness.

Lambda: An ancient Greek symbol representing unity. It's been widely adopted as a symbol of LGBTQ+ rights, including at the International Gay Rights Congress in 1974 and by organizations like Lambda Legal and Lambda Literary.

Flowers: Flowers and plants including pansies, lavender, carnations, and violets have all been used as slang, signaling, or reclaimed terminology for queer people over time. For example, Oscar Wilde popularized the green carnation as a symbol of gay identity in the 1890s when he asked his friends to wear green carnations at the premiere of *Lady Windermere's Fan*, creating a secret code for men who loved men.

Inverted triangles: Once used as a marker for gay men persecuted by the Nazis, the pink inverted triangle has been reclaimed by gay liberation organizations like ACT UP to symbolize the way the AIDS epidemic was taking the lives of so many queer people.

2018: *Pose* on FX sets a record for the most transgender actors featured regularly in a scripted series, including cast members Angelica Ross, Dominique Jackson, Hailie Sahar, Indya Moore, and Michaela Jaé Rodriguez.

2020: Netflix releases *Disclosure: Trans Lives on Screen*, which documents the impact of Hollywood on trans peoples' lives, careers, and public visibility.

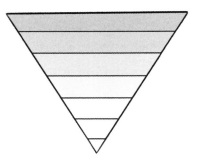

"Young people have always been at the forefront of these movements. They expand our horizons of what freedom looks and feels like. They develop and practice political strategies and forms of dissent that make movements dream bigger. So often these contributions remain unnoticed or unremarkable because young people are institutionally gatekept from decision making and spheres of influence."
—ALOK Vaid-Menon

ALOK VAID-MENON
(THEY/THEM)

ALOK is an author, speaker, poet, and comedian who is fighting for beauty. They say, "Alongside being gender nonconforming, I'm also genre nonconforming. *Artist* is the word that I feel most at home in. It's elastic, which means it can hold all the various ways that I orbit around the world. It also speaks to the need to *create* alternate ways of living, loving, and looking. That's where I'm at now: a desire to create something different. I think I also like the word because of its association with beauty. It's not just what I'm fighting against (like the gender binary), it's what I'm fighting for: beauty."

ALOK sees themself first and foremost as a love poet. They say, "I'm just trying to bring love everywhere I go, to everything I do." They currently travel the world sharing that love with communities by speaking and sharing their internationally acclaimed poetry. While in college, ALOK cofounded DarkMatter with a friend, creating a trans South Asian performance art duo, which toured their performances and workshops with a specific emphasis on calling out the lack of representation of South Asian queer and trans poets.

After graduating college, ALOK moved to New York City, where they began working with the Audre Lorde Project, a community organizing center for LGBTQIA+ BIPOC. They say, "As a young person, ALP was my political and creative home and taught me so much that I still hold dear to me now, especially a commitment to cultural work as political work. Now, my biggest inspirations are my peers: transfeminine BIPOC artists across the world I've had the pleasure of collaborating with throughout the years. People like Travis Alabanza and Shea Diamond."

Books bring ALOK peace and comfort, and they've recently started posting book reports on their Instagram to share their learning with others around topics like the racist history of how people view body hair, or trans people's access to health care, or Black trans leaders from history. They've also published books including *Femme in Public* (2017), *Beyond the Gender Binary* (2020), and *Your Wound/My Garden* (2021).

ALOK is very proud of recently delivering the keynote for Creating Change, an annual LGBTQ rights conference hosted by the Task Force, which they attended as a young queer/trans person. "It was foundational [in those early years] in connecting me with ideas and people that totally transformed my life and helped me come into myself," they say. "It felt like a full-circle moment to be able to share my art in this forum." In their speech, they talked about how their journey of self-love and self-acceptance is increasingly teaching them the potent potential of love—and how choosing love over fear can and will change the world. ALOK credits this spirit of possibility to their maasi (aunt), Urvashi Vaid, a well-loved lesbian activist and attorney who has always been a role model to them.

In envisioning the future, ALOK says, "I want to continue to show up as my full self: flawed, contradictory, wonderful. I want to continue to explore who I am and get closer and closer to living my most authentic life. I want to be a good friend to the people I love. I want to cultivate joy, hope, and wonder in everything I do."

"Everyone expects queer youth to be the future and that's absolutely the truth. However, there's maturing that we should be able to do later in our lives that we're being forced to do now. So, it's difficult. We are the future, but we're also kids, and I should be able to learn from older folks around me." —Ella McKenzie

ELLA MCKENZIE
(SHE/HER)

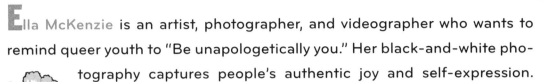

Ella McKenzie is an artist, photographer, and videographer who wants to remind queer youth to "Be unapologetically you." Her black-and-white photography captures people's authentic joy and self-expression. Ella's first book, *Silenced*, features photos and interviews with LGBTQ youth in New York. She says, "Writing my book is what helped me realize that I'm a learner. My perspective on queerness, being a person of color, or my perspective and outlook on life in general is different to other people. I don't know everything." Ella believes that approaching art and activism with curiosity is the best way to learn and expand our understanding of what it means to be human.

Silenced began when Ella's high school was offering grants to fund meaningful projects. Ella felt angry about anti-trans bills attempting to ban gender-affirming health care, and wanted to find a way to uplift and celebrate the stories of trans youth. She received a grant and headed to a local drag show to connect with friends. From there, friends told other friends, and soon enough Ella was holding a six-hour photo shoot with thirty-five young people who lived in New York. Ella laid out the photos paired with stories from written interviews with each of the young people—noting things like their favorite musicians, their coming-out stories, and their hopes for the future. She says, "It was so great meeting all these kids and hearing their stories." Now Ella wants to expand the project to other states and cities, like Boston, Baton Rouge, Los Angeles, and Florida.

Photography brings Ella so much joy because she gets to do something she loves but that also tells stories. In collaboration with the Future

Perfect Project, Ella is finding other mediums in which to tell stories too, like podcasts. She's currently recording a podcast centering trans queer joy with topics spanning healthy relationships, examining queer television like *Heartstopper*, and positive affirmations. Between photo shoots and school, she loves hanging out with her baby sister and exploring her creativity through playing the ukulele.

In learning about other youths' experiences, Ella has been able to learn more about her own experience of gender identity and expression too. She's proud of recently painting her nails, which felt like a big deal, because she says, "I've been trying to move with this

PHOTOGRAPHY COLLECTIONS: BOOKS AND WEBSITES

AMERICAN BOYS | Soraya Zaman, Daylight Books, 2019

ARE YOU OK? (areyouokportraits.com) | Jesse Freidin, Self-published, 2023

BEYOND MAGENTA: Transgender Teens Speak Out | Susan Kuklin, Candlewick, 2014

FEARLESS: Portraits of LGBT Student Athletes | Jeff Sheng, Somebody Books, 2015

PRIDE PORTRAITS (instagram.com/prideportraits) | Eden Rose Torres

QUEER LOVE IN COLOR | Jamal Jordan, Ten Speed Press, 2021

TO SURVIVE ON THIS SHORE | Jess T. Dugan and Vanessa Fabbre, Kehrer Verlag, 2018

TRANSCENDING SELF | (transcending-self.com) | Annie Tritt

WE ARE HERE: Visionaries of Color Transforming the Art World | Jasmin Hernandez, Abrams, 2021

WE ARE THE YOUTH | Laurel Golio and Diana Scholl, Space-Made, 2014

slogan of embracing my femininity and enhancing my mas-culinity. I think for a lot of mascs, it's hard for us to kind of embrace our femininity because we don't want to come off as weak, or maybe it confuses us a little bit because of these gender norms that society has created, and so getting my nails painted is such a big deal, because it's something that I avoided for so long because I thought that it was such a feminine thing to do. I've just been trying to kind of work on that so that's something that I'm pretty proud of that's on a lesser scale."

Ella is energized by other artists and storytellers, includ-ing Zanele Muholi, a nonbinary photographer from South Africa; Frank Ocean, a Black bisexual musician; Celeste Lecesne, the cofounder of the Trevor Project and Future Perfect Project; and her friend Maliyah, who has a queer clothing brand. Her favorite show of all time is *Pose*, and she admires the amazingly tal-ented cast. Seeing each of these creators be their full selves and center youth experiences is meaningful to Ella, and it provides ongoing motivation to continue doing the similarly powerful work she's doing.

"Young people are the heartbeat."
—Jess Guilbeaux

JESS GUILBEAUX
(SHE/HER)

Jess Guilbeaux is a public speaker, model, and self-described tech nerd who believes in practicing "action-first activism." She grew up in the small city of Lawrence, Kansas, where she came out at sixteen. She says, "As a Black queer woman, especially coming from where I come from, living out and proud is activism within itself." Jess experienced a painful coming-out process with her adoptive parents, which led to homelessness. Her best friend, Carmen, gave her a place to stay. "Without my chosen family, without my foundational friends, I don't know where I would be. I wouldn't be here." It was a process for Jess, though, to redefine family and believe she could have a strong chosen family to rely on. Carmen nominated Jess for *Queer Eye*, during which Jess says she had her "queer coming of age" and was able not only to grow into her queerness and identity but also to realize that "family is whatever we make of it."

In the episode titled "Black Girl Magic" of *Queer Eye*'s third season, Jess explored identity, family, self-confidence, and community alongside the Fab Five. She reconnected with her biological sister, learned about the history of her family's genealogy, and celebrated all the members of the chosen family she'd built over the years. In a visit to the Kansas City Friends of Alvin Ailey dance studio with Karamo Brown, Jess learned more about her community's resources and affirmed, "I am a strong Black lesbian woman."

The Fab Five continues to be a support system for Jess, and she also finds incredible support and strength from local community organizers in Kansas. "Back in my small town, the ones who are still doing what they can

with very little . . . those are the people who I look to for determination, perseverance," she says. Cody Keith Charles, founder and executive director of Haus of McCoy—a queer and trans community center in Lawrence, Kansas—is one organizer Jess reaches out to for advice.

Since moving to Philadelphia in 2021 for her first internship, Jess has been focused on activism through partnerships with impactful organizations, while also finishing her degree in computer science to become a "future tech genius!" Like many students, Jess struggled with student loan debt when first entering college and decided to drop out. She's now back in school and thrilled to soon have a degree. Outside of studying and working at her internship, Jess has partnered with companies and Pride celebrations to uplift the work of organizations like the Future Perfect Project, a nonprofit creating safe spaces for youth to connect through the arts, as well as the Okra Project, a collective providing home-cooked meals to Black trans people.

Jess finds lots of joy in spending time with her girlfriend, cat, and dog—"a cute little quad family," as they call it. She also loves listening to music and has a tattoo of a lyric from the song "Last Hope" by Paramore, her favorite band. Jess spends a lot of time with the drag performer community in Philadelphia—and used to perform drag herself back in Kansas. "It just brings me so much joy to take other friends and new people that I meet, and I'm like, come on—we're going to my favorite place. We're going to drag and we're going to have a good time and smile and laugh!" Jess's community and chosen family have brought her so much love and safety, and she enjoys sharing in return through her activism and friendship.

"I've always found that young people are the
most invested in change-making, because we're
the ones that are going to be living in the
world we're fighting so hard to change."
—Joshua Allen

JOSHUA ALLEN
(THEY/THEM)

Joshua Allen is an artist, activist, change-maker, and cultural creator. Growing up in a family of community organizers in Brooklyn, New York, meant that there wasn't a "before activism" for Joshua—they have always organized for a better future. Their work as an abolitionist acknowledges how state violence harms Black, Indigenous, and trans people, and uplifts the importance of solidarity across movements for liberation.

In June 2020, they helped organize and co-host the Brooklyn Liberation March, which became the largest documented protest for Black trans lives in US history; over fifteen thousand people marched through the streets of Brooklyn with protest signs exclaiming "Protect Trans Youth" and "Black Trans Lives Are Sacred." A coalition of people and organizations came together to make this action happen, including the Black Excellence Collective (which Joshua founded and directs), the Okra Project, the Marsha P. Johnson Institute, GLITS, For the Gworls, and Black Trans Femmes in the Arts. Joshua says the action was organized because "a lot of us in the LGBTQ community—particularly people who are nonbinary, gender nonconforming, and trans—had felt like so many of the stories of violence, police brutality, and the overall culture of violence have fallen extremely harshly on Black trans people, and that there's been a disproportionate amount of attention and an unfair economy of care around what stories are uplifted, what stories are pointed out in the media, and then which ones are ignored."

Through protest—and also through art and photography—Joshua has many mediums for telling authentic human stories. They create portraits to document the African diaspora, queerness, love, addiction, romance, relationships, and culture. In 2020, their art series *Returning Home* debuted. Art, music, dancing, and traveling bring so much joy to Joshua's life, especially in the ways that each of those things allows them to learn about culture, language, food, heritage, and humanity.

When asked what is most important to acknowledge in their story, Joshua shares that "every accomplishment I've had in my life, every exciting thing that I've ever done, it's been supported by a village of people who make me greater. It takes a village to do anything important or powerful or game-changing, and none of this, the work that I do, would be possible without the people who are there with me holding me up, believing in me, and [who] saw me before I could really see myself." Aside from their family, their greatest heroes are Miss Major, who has been a mentor to them over the years, as well as writers and activists Angela Davis, Bayard Rustin, and James Baldwin.

"I struggled so much with my gender and sexuality
growing up, so I've taken those experiences
and chosen to share them with the rest of the
world in hopes that I'll help someone feel seen,
heard, represented, and loved." —Meg Lee

MEG LEE
(THEY/THEM)

Meg Lee is an artist and activist whose work is centered around their "love for creativity, art, expression, self-love, and activism." Through their vibrant, affirming illustrations on Instagram (@megemikoart), Meg can express themself freely and unapologetically, which is something they longed for as a child and young adult. By sharing their experiences of being Asian American and trans nonbinary, as well as designing educational content about anti-trans legislation, Meg's goal is to "create a safer and more accepting world for *all* trans folks and trans kids."

What Meg is most proud of is their collaborations with other trans activists, including Schuyler Bailar (whom you'll read more about in chapter 3, "Educators"). Meg and Schuyler teamed up to create an apparel design with the purpose of raising funds to fight anti-trans sports bills and bans. Meg says, "This was a really exciting collaboration and project for me, as Schuyler is someone who I've been inspired by for so many years. To become friends and to work so closely on a project that means so much to both of us was such a wholesome and amazing experience for me."

Meg also recently had the opportunity to work with Fenty, Rihanna's beauty brand, and felt proud of being able to create the representation they needed as a young person. They say, "Being able to film myself for Fenty and have it seen on social media for other Asian American trans nonbinary folks to see was something that made my current and younger self so proud."

Much of Meg's work is inspired by their grandma Bess, who motivates them to "follow my heart and to create a life for myself that I enjoy living

in." Their grandma was an artist who had to give up her dreams of making art her career after she and her family came back from being incarcerated in the Japanese American concentration camps during World War II. Meg says, "Although I lost her in 2019, she is still someone who I think of daily. I always hope that the work that I'm doing is making her proud." Meg's parents are also an incredibly meaningful part of Meg's life, as they've given Meg unconditional love, support, and pride. Meg says, "This is an important part of my story because they have created a safe space at home for me to be my true self."

Meg finds so much joy in being outside in the sun. They say, "Since top surgery, I have so much more confidence and love being able to wear all the clothes I couldn't wear before I got top surgery. This has really opened up so many new doors for me and has allowed me to truly be me somewhere other than in the safety of my home." Aside from basking in the sun, Meg's absolute favorite activity is playing fetch with their dog, Lilo, and spending time with their partner, Kai. Meg says, "Kai has been by my side since the very beginning of my journey exploring my gender. She has not only supported me through every bump in the road, but she also continues to fight for the trans community by educating others and standing with me when I don't have the energy or capacity to go up against all the transphobia alone. When I got top surgery, she was there throughout my entire recovery and continues to do everything she can to make our home a safe and loving environment."

In the coming years, Meg envisions a life of growth and collaboration, and says, "Whether that be through continuing to share my personal journey, raising money, or working on more projects, I hope that the work I do helps as many LGBTQIA+ folks and QTBIPOC as possible."

"I want to tell a younger version of myself that my story is worth something. My experience matters."
—Reeves Gift

REEVES GIFT
(HE/HIM)

Reeves Gift is a filmmaker and writer who describes his work as striving to heal the world through bridge building. He says, "I like telling stories about rural masculinity. There's a lot of really unique stories that can be told there." He approaches his work with the intention of telling the truth, rather than crafting narratives that neatly fit. He says, "It's not fair for us, as marginalized people, to have to defeat stereotypes or be the most morally upstanding hero. I create stories about marginalized people who are not perfect." Reeves most recently worked on story development for *Euphoria*, seasons six and seven of *Big Mouth* at HBO, and season two of *Human Resources*. His personal film projects and photography have been supported by Los Angeles County, PBS SoCal, and public schools in California.

In high school, Reeves found joy in playing soccer, serving on student government, and spending time with his supportive friends. Unfortunately, Reeves's parents didn't offer the same support, and he became homeless. With the care of his friends, he pushed through his senior year (when he was named homecoming king) and received a full-ride scholarship to attend the University of Southern California in Los Angeles. College would allow Reeves to connect with a new community, as well as pursue his dreams of filmmaking.

In college, Reeves ran support groups at the LGBT Center and created films that he's incredibly proud of. One of those films highlighted young people's experiences with the foster care system. He says, "I think that there are a lot of characters in film and television who live on the margins and rise to the top. I want to tell a younger version of myself that my story is worth something. My experience matters." He also developed a special that aired in Germany featuring intergenerational conversations about LGBTQ+ people. In those discussions, Reeves explored his experiences as a young Caribbean Black person at this moment in history and the ways movements for liberation have evolved over time.

In 2018, Reeves was awarded the Youth Leadership Award from SMYAL, an LGBTQ+ empowerment organization that offers scholarships to student leaders every year. The following year, he was named a Point Foundation Scholar and joined a network of LGBTQ+ students receiving support for their education. In the annual announcement of Point Foundation Scholars, Reeves shared, "I want to take the tools education gives me to make change in the displacement of Black and Indigenous queer people of color. I know nothing will begin unless I use my voice, and nothing will change unless I move."

As Reeves has grown as an artist and a person, he says his focus and values have shifted toward speaking to people who are indifferent or don't have access to learning about trans communities. "There's a huge geographical divide," he says. Reeves wants to see greater emphasis on the needs of rural communities. "Many people haven't met a transgender person before. I want to write stories that can inform and persuade and bring humor to trans narratives. I want to use the tools I have to challenge all those hardwired views and have really good conversations with people."

Alongside creating films and art, Reeves finds joy in spending time with his cat, "a basketball-shaped beauty named Malcolm," boxing, power-lifting, and baking macaroons.

"Stay true, stay you."
—Ryan Cassata

RYAN CASSATA
(HE/HIM)

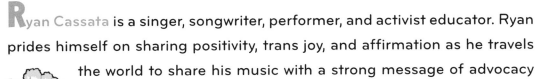

Ryan Cassata is a singer, songwriter, performer, and activist educator. Ryan prides himself on sharing positivity, trans joy, and affirmation as he travels the world to share his music with a strong message of advocacy and gender inclusivity.

Ryan grew up on Long Island, New York, and began his work as an activist at the age of thirteen when he joined the LGBT Network's Safe Schools Team. By speaking publicly at schools and online through vlogs, Ryan has opened people's hearts and minds—especially young people's. He says, "I think that people underestimate the power of youth, and when I was a young teenager, I was already an activist, and I would go into schools and talk to people the same age as me, and I would be able to change their minds from transphobia and bigotry to supporting trans people. I think part of that reason was because I was the same age. So it was peer to peer."

When Ryan first began speaking and posting videos online, it was hard to find many other trans guys in the media. He says that Joe Stevens, guitarist of progressive country band Coyote Grace, impacted him most early on. Ryan says, "He's an out trans guy, and he was touring the country to play music on an acoustic guitar like I do. And I discovered him when I was fourteen, and it was the first time that I saw a trans guy doing what I wanted to do when I grew up, and being able to do it. When I came out, I thought it was like, 'Oh, well I'm not able to do anything in my life,' and I saw Joe and I felt like there was hope. He was my lighthouse. I showed my parents his videos, and that helped me to realize being trans isn't a death sentence. When I was eighteen, I finally got to meet him, and

we've been buddies ever since." Ryan's other influences include Lucas Silveira and StormMiguel Florez.

Ryan has made so many ground-breaking achievements, including being the first openly trans performer at the Vans Warped Tour and the youngest keynote speaker at the Philadelphia Trans Wellness conference. His powerful songs, like "Daughter," "Hold On—You Belong," and "Queer Love Outlaw" center stories of trans and queer joy, acceptance, and love. His performances create space for young people to feel connected and

HARVEY MILK

Ryan shares something in common with one of the most well-known gay activists of the past century. In 1977, Harvey Milk became the first openly gay person to be elected to public office in California, making gay history. Both Harvey Milk and Ryan Cassata graduated from Bay Shore High School in Bay Shore, New York.

During Milk's lifetime, he made a historic impact and understood the risks of being an openly gay activist. As an elected member of the San Francisco Board of Supervisors in the late 1970s, Milk was instrumental in passing a gay rights ordinance for the city prohibiting anti-gay discrimination in employment and housing. Only eleven months after his election, in 1978, Harvey Milk was assassinated.

Ryan decided to commemorate Harvey Milk by getting a tattoo of one of Milk's famous quotes for his eighteenth birthday: "If a bullet should enter my brain, let that bullet destroy every closet door." Ryan became the first-ever recipient of the Harvey Milk Memorial Award from his high school in 2011.

"HOPE WILL NEVER BE SILENT."

"ALL YOUNG PEOPLE, REGARDLESS OF SEXUAL ORIENTATION OR IDENTITY, DESERVE A SAFE AND SUPPORTIVE ENVIRONMENT IN WHICH TO ACHIEVE THEIR FULL POTENTIAL."

—HARVEY MILK

cared for. He says, "Just seeing audiences smiling and singing so proudly about being trans warms my heart." Ryan signed a record deal in 2023 with Kill Rock Stars, a label known for iconic rock musicians like the Decemberists, Elliott Smith, and Bikini Kill.

Ryan is currently in graduate school for a Master of Divinity and Master of Art and Social Transformation. He's given sermons about queer love and healing from religious trauma, which has become an important part of his activism and social justice work. Healing is at the center of much of his work, especially creating healing spaces for trans youth and inviting them to "hold on" and live full lives. He recently traveled to San Antonio, Texas, to provide support to youth and families there, where he says, "They need that love and support. They want to see an older trans person out there doing their thing and being happy and successful. It's really empowering."

"I believe that younger generations just find the vocabulary for things that prior generations could not. Youth will bring through things that older generations are afraid to do."
—Sara K. Dunn

SARA K. DUNN
(SHE/HER)

Sara K. Dunn is a queer multimedia artist and budding ecologist whose creations explore queerness, emotion, and interconnectivity through the lens of her queer, neurodivergent, and feminist identities. Through her art-making, Sara hopes to uplift voices, realities, and stories that were once silenced or underrepresented in art through her multimedia practice.

One of the big themes in Sara's art is embracing and exploring her own queerness. She was raised in a Catholic military family that moved around a lot; they lived in Germany when Sara was ten to eighteen years old. These experiences, she says, "stunted realizing that I was queer. I didn't come out as queer or really accept myself until I was twenty-two. So it took me a while, and I definitely did queer acts, or fell in love with people, but I didn't know how to acknowledge it or accept it. Growing up in those environments suppressed me, and I didn't want to explore things because I was afraid."

When she was nineteen, Sara started an Instagram account, and that's mainly where she likes to share her creations. She says, "I find it's a way to share my work that's not such a formal space as a portfolio website. I feel like people love to see the process and the person behind the work." She was featured in a gallery show called *Homage* at On the Fringe in New York City in March 2022. The show was curated by Toni Smalls, a friend of Sara's who is a Black trans artist, curator, and poet. At the show, Sara displayed her sculptures, all about processing grief. Each figure represented different motions of grief—sitting in it, absorbing it, feeling it fully, reflecting it.

Another major aspect of Sara's art is focused on making meaningful political statements about who is represented in works of art. She says, "I try to represent figures that have not been represented much, like people of different body sizes or identities that were just not shown in whitewashed history. I'm also interested in ethical art practices and creating responsibly, and also how my work is reactive to the contemporary world and the people around it. Art is not created in the capsule." Sara cares deeply about how she creates her art, and the message it sends to the world.

Spending time with her friends and loved ones brings Sara so much joy—as well as going on research tangents! Whether it's learning about external pockets that women wore in the seventeenth century, collecting antique objects, or exploring and caring for gardens, Sara loves embracing her curiosity and learning about the past. She's fascinated and inspired by Edna W. Lawrence, the founder of the Nature Lab at Rhode Island School of Design (RISD), a lesbian naturalist who lived with her partner for over fifty years. Sara is working on a children's book about Edna's life. She hopes to create many children's picture books, and eventually graphic novels. She says, "I see so many things that I want to create and share. I am in grad school for art and ecology in Ireland in hopes of becoming a professor in tandem with my art practice." She dreams about creating public installations of her sculptures—ones that are functional and interactive, like enormous pothos leaves providing shade at bus stops.

"As a contemporary artist, I feel like I have a responsibility to create art that thoughtfully considers current social and environmental conditions. Whether it is creating illustrations that respectfully and accurately depict people of all walks of life, or crafting sculptures with unexpected recyclables that give them a new life, I am creating with a conscious mind. It's important to be considerate of the world around you, while also creating a world that you would like to see within your art. As an artist, you are an innovator, a creative curious mind, a dreamer, a builder of potential futures. Do not doubt the impact that your artwork can have."
—Sara K. Dunn

"Youth play a huge role in really transforming the future for us, and their voices are underestimated, and also highly overlooked. Whether it's protesting or organizing campaigns, or whatever medium you choose—art, poetry—there's a lot of different ways of expressing that." —Shannon Li

SHANNON LI
(SHE/HER & THEY/THEM)

Shannon Li is a designer and advocate grounded in intersectionality, accessibility, and inclusion. Through their work as a designer and activist, Shannon says they want to "be able to be a representation for other queer youth out there, specifically queer youth of color. Because I know the challenges that come with sharing these identities. Just to be able to set an example and inspiration and be a resource for them as well, if they don't have that resource within the area or the community that they live in."

Shannon's time with the GLAAD Campus Ambassador program has been formative in shaping her work as an artist and activist. Through GLAAD, Shannon was able to publish their personal narratives and attend Pride in New York. She says GLAAD gave her "a lot of opportunities within queer advocacy, and a platform for me to voice my opinions, which will also be a voice for other queer youth." In 2019, Shannon had the opportunity to design a shirt for Lucky Brand's Pride Capsule Collection as part of their "Lucky x Love" campaign. Their design was focused on the freedom to be ourselves and the empowerment of LGBTQ+ communities.

Shannon is also working to change the design world, and envisions a more accessible and inclusive future for designers. Shannon works in product design, or user experience design, and is pushing forward participatory design that considers everyone's needs. This means involving communities directly in the design and research process, like a community health access initiative that Shannon is working on with LGBTQ+ youth in the Michigan area. They hope to create a centralized site for health care resources for youth who might be struggling to find access within their area. Shannon also thinks a lot about accessibility for disabled folks in her work, and wants to move the design world beyond checklists of inclusion. These standards often miss the nuance of people's unique needs. Through participatory design, Shannon hopes to create more access and support.

Shannon finds lots of joy in indie pop and rock music and says, "It's such a good way of connecting with people and really expressing my own emotions, and I honestly would consider it like my best friend. You can have that flexibility choosing your favorite songs, and what you resonate with. I personally love music. I've been trying to go to more concerts, and it's just a good environment to be in a space where people enjoy the same artist as you do." Shannon also loves being by the water—at coastline beaches and waterfronts just relaxing and taking in nature.

UX DESIGN ACCESSIBILITY

"User experience design is how humans interact with technology and the continuous design improvements of those experiences. Oftentimes, designers compromise accessibility for designs that are aesthetically beautiful. While visual design is incredibly important for designers, it shouldn't render digital products to be inaccessible. Designers do not think enough about how they can design for disabled individuals that may have visual impairments, cognitive disabilities, physical disabilities, and much more. This means in addition to checking color contrast ratios are met, font size is large enough, spacing is adequate between items, and much more, it is important to also work with disability communities on design projects to better understand their lived experiences and how we can design for and with them."

—Shannon Li

BOOKS ABOUT DISABILITY JUSTICE

CARE WORK: Dreaming Disability Justice | Leah Lakshmi Piepzna-
   Samarasinha, Arsenal Pulp, 2018

CRIP KINSHIP: The Disability Justice & Art Activism of Sins Invalid |
   Shayda Kafai, Arsenal Pulp, 2021

*DEMYSTIFYING DISABILITY: What to Know, What to Say, and How to Be an
   Ally* | Emily Ladau, Ten Speed, 2021

DISABILITY VISIBILITY: First-Person Stories from the Twenty-First Century
   | Ed. Alice Wong, Vintage, 2020

*FIGHTING FOR YES!: The Story of Disability Rights Activist Judith
   Heumann* | Maryann Cocca-Leffler, illustrated by Vivien Mildenberger,
   Abrams Books for Young Readers, 2022

THE FUTURE IS DISABLED: Prophecies, Love Notes, and Mourning | Leah
   Lakshmi Piepzna-Samarasinha, Arsenal Pulp, 2022

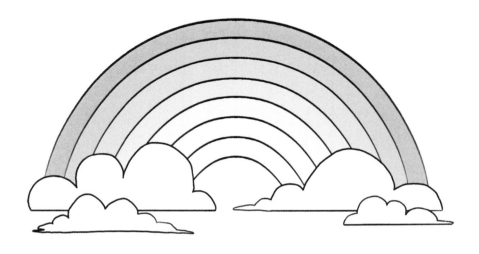

"It's so important for us all to keep imagining this collective future together. Everyone's perspective is needed. The gender binary sucks, and we need to eradicate it! Not just for nonbinary people, not just for trans people, but for everybody." —Somah Haaland

SOMAH HAALAND
(THEY/THEM)

Somah Haaland is a queer and nonbinary artist and organizer from the pueblos of Laguna and Jemez. Somah has a deep love for nature and for connecting playfully with the natural world, which motivates much of their work and their vision for the future. In reflecting on the goal of their work, they say, "That's the whole point of all this liberation work. We're fighting the roots of colonization that are oppressing so many people. The whole point is so that we can just be human beings that enjoy living on this earth, because we are a part of it, and we are a part of nature."

They're a media organizer for Pueblo Action Alliance, a grassroots organization in Southern Tiwa territory (Albuquerque, New Mexico), which promotes cultural sustainability and community defense in Indigenous communities. This femme Two-Spirit matriarch-led organization energizes Somah every day. They say that working alongside other queer Indigenous people helps them know that they're not alone, and it motivates them to continue the important work of building community and protecting the land.

In 2022, Somah narrated the film *Our Story: The Indigenous Led Fight to Protect Greater Chaco*, which is a call to action to save the remaining 9 percent of lands stewarded by Indigenous peoples in the Greater Chaco—the sacred homelands of Pueblo and Diné people. These sites are of utmost importance to Indigenous peoples, and are at risk of being lost to oil and gas extraction. Somah's mother, Deb Haaland, is also featured in *Our Story*. Deb Haaland was a US Representative for New Mexico's 1st

DEB HAALAND

Secretary Deb Haaland, an enrolled member of the Puebla of Laguna and thirty-fifth-generation New Mexican, was the first Native American person to become Secretary of the Interior. This made history and holds a lot of meaning, because the Secretary of the Interior is the person responsible for managing all federal policy that impacts the 574 federally recognized tribal nations, in addition to national parks. That means that, in the past, non-Indigenous people made decisions about tribal nations' relationships with the US government through the Bureau of Indian Affairs, leading to harmful policies that stripped Indigenous people of their lands and caused both physical and cultural violence, including genocide. Secretary Haaland's appointment creates greater possibility and opportunity for Indigenous people to impact decisions directly affecting them.

congressional district, and in 2021 was named Secretary of the Interior, becoming the first Indigenous person appointed to the post.

Film, theater, photography, and poetry bring Somah an abundance of joy, especially in the ways that each of these creative expressions allows for human connection and storytelling. They say, "I think poetry ties into this bigger theme of storytelling. Indigenous people are storytellers by nature, you know, so much of our traditions are passed down orally, and not through writing, so there's stories that have survived with my ancestors through generations. And it's a way that we relate to each other as humans." One of Somah's greatest inspirations is ALOK (also featured in this chapter, page 90), who describes people as living poems. Somah says they aspire to live their life as a living poem too.

Somah is also passionate about uplifting youth through creative expression and building safe spaces. While teaching theater classes and working at Circo Latino at the National Hispanic Cultural Center, Somah worked with young people who said they felt like they had finally found a space to be themselves. When Somah was in high school, they were very active with their school's GSA, which similarly gave them space to explore their queerness and find supportive friends. In all of Somah's work, they say, "I bring my queerness into every aspect of the things that I do. It's taken me a while to get to the point where I can no longer emotionally afford to check my queerness at the door when I enter spaces, so I'm gonna bring it into my work." Now, as an adult working with youth, they can authentically share their queerness and artistic perspective, which creates spaces for young people to unapologetically be their full selves too.

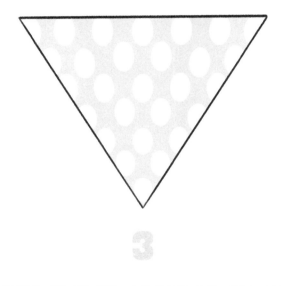

3

EDUCATORS

When was the first time you learned about LGBTQ+ people in an educational setting? Not from friends or family, but in an educational space like a classroom or school. What did you learn? Do you remember what the messages were, and how you felt learning about LGBTQ+ people? Was it a positive experience?

Artists and community organizers have the opportunity to express their messages through education. Bringing people together for a support group, holding a protest, or creating a social media graphic about trans history: all these forms of activism bring greater understanding and education to the people they reach. Educators in particular can dedicate their advocacy efforts to finding creative and effective ways to open people's hearts and minds by sharing their experiences and working toward a better educational system. They might pair their education work with advocacy and organizing work as well because there are so many policies that impact education and the key issues that these educators focus on.

Many lead workshops and presentations for teachers, administrators, student leaders, companies, and more. For instance, when Sameer Jha was fourteen years old, they founded the Empathy Alliance, which has now

ULTIMATELY, THE GOAL OF OFFERING EDUCATION WAS TO PROVIDE SAFETY.

reached over one million educators across the country. By speaking directly with teachers, Sameer is able to "educate the educators" and improve schools for LGBTQ youth.

Some advocate for changes to education policy, like improving sexual health education or requiring LGBTQ-inclusive curriculum. Rebekah Bruesehoff, for example, testified before her state legislature in New Jersey to require schools to include the accomplishments and contributions of LGBTQ people, as well as disabled people, across all disciplines in the curriculum. So far, only six states have passed similar bills (California, Colorado, Illinois, Oregon, and Nevada). Rebekah advocates for the needs of young people to be seen in their curriculum, so they can show up as their full selves at school and learn about their own histories and bodies.

Educators find impactful ways to share their ideas with bigger audiences, like creating videos on TikTok about intersex history (Mari Wrobi), writing books about inclusion and self-expression (Trinity Neal and Desi Napoles), or posting informational guides on Instagram to debunk misinformation (Schuyler Bailar). They've all designed meaningful educational tools that influence individuals, schools, towns, and the larger society.

STUDENTS TRANSFORMING SCHOOLS

Gender-Sexuality Alliances (GSAs), formerly called Gay-Straight Alliances, are spaces for students to build community with each other, take action on important issues, and educate their schools about LGBTQ inclusion. Simply having a GSA improves overall school climate and reduces derogatory comments about LGBTQ people. These student-led, adult-supported groups are foundational to the shifts we've seen in schools over the past fifty years. The earliest documented college-based group started in 1970 at Columbia University, and the first secondary-school-based group began at New York City's George Washington High School in 1972.

Until 2007, the narrative had long been that the first GSA was founded in 1989 at Concord Academy, an elite, private, majority-white school in Massachusetts. It was the first to be named a Gay-Straight Alliance. However, Dominique Johnson, a researcher for the Joseph Beam Youth Collaborative, discovered the demands of the George Washington High School group, which was led by students of color in the Bronx almost two decades before, and published their story in 2007 in the journal *Children, Youth and Environments*. They had demanded their rights to form a group, to be included in the sexuality curriculum, and to see all homophobic materials removed from their schools. The group had been proposed by an eighteen-year-old student, Elie Lamadrid, and approved by faculty member Alexander Levie.

On the West Coast, Dr. Virginia Uribe created Project 10 twelve years later at Fairfax High School in Los Angeles, California. Project 10 is a

YOUTH LIBERATION PRESS

LGBTQ young people also provided education to the wider public by circulating publications, pamphlets, and zines, like the 1976 pamphlet *Growing Up Gay*, published by Youth Liberation Press in the Ann Arbor magazine *FPS: A Magazine of Young People's Liberation*. It featured articles from youth perspectives on the topics of coming out, starting gay groups, and dealing with family. An article titled "George Washington Goes Gay" chronicled the development of "George Washington High School's new gay group." On the next page, you can read an excerpt of the students' demands.

OUR DEMANDS*

The school system is oppressive to all who are forced to participate in it. Among these people are gay students, who either must hide or who are just coming out—in constant fear of being discovered.

And since the high school is a microcosm of society in general, gay students are expected to keep their self-identity buried under the unfounded and senseless prejudices of their "authorities" and prejudices which are based upon backward social, political and economic ideas. If a student is found out to be gay, he or she will most probably be rushed to the dean, have his or her parents called, and all hell will break loose.

But gay people will no longer tolerate this oppression. Throughout the world, gays are rising up and demanding their just and true rights as humans beings. Recognizing the power and function of independent liberation movements, gays have learned much from the black liberation movement and the women's liberation movement, and have created the gay liberation movement.

Therefore, we as gay students demand the same rights (social and political) as "straight" students.

Therefore, we make the following demands upon the city high schools of New York:

1. The right to form gay groups of both a social and political nature.
2. The right to be included and to receive fair representation in any high school course dealing with sexuality (as both sexual beings and as a political movement in a changing society with changing cultural values), and if none exist, to have them created.
3. The right to be treated as equal human beings, which includes the removal of all textbooks and other educational media that treat homosexuality as an aberration, rather than as an integral and important part of human sexuality.

*"George Washington Goes Gay." *Growing Up Gay: A Youth Liberation Pamphlet*, no. 54 (Ann Arbor, MI: Youth Liberation Press, 1976), 20–24.

reference to the statistic at the time that about 10 percent of the population is gay. Dr. Uribe was known for supporting and uplifting Black students, which also made her a safe adult for LGBT students to reach out to. Alongside her students, she founded the first program in the country meant to address and prevent the high dropout rates of gay, lesbian, and bisexual youth. Dr. Uribe made history not only by founding the program, but also by later being one of the first educators in her district to come out publicly.

Black and Latine students and educators have long been at the forefront of the movement and deserve to be similarly centered in histories about movements for liberation. Of course there are many stories that have gone untold and there will be much more work in uncovering those histories and better documenting new ones as they emerge.

So what happened in the earliest years of LGBTQ students organizing publicly within their schools? Education, of course! But ultimately, the goal of offering education was to provide safety. Dr. Uribe's students came to her because they felt unsafe and were experiencing bullying. GSAs offer a brave, supportive space for students to simply be themselves without fear of harassment from their peers in the larger school. This safety net helps build confidence and leads to bigger, more public actions, like creating a list of demands for administrators to improve a school, or speaking out publicly to the media or local legislators.

In 1980, BAGLY launched the very first LGBTQ youth speakers bureau, which brought LGBTQ people into public schools to speak with classes and facilitate assemblies. This historic program paved the way for many educational initiatives to come in later years and emphasized the importance of people hearing directly from LGBTQ people about their experiences in order to build empathy and understanding. It provided opportunities for educators and students to undo the stigma and shame they'd learned about LGBTQ communities by asking questions and listening to stories. Mari Wrobi, one of the educators featured in this chapter, says: "I share my story about being nonbinary, about being trans, about being queer, and education is really where my passion lies, because I am comfortable with questions that otherwise might be considered inappropriate or uncomfortable." To help educators understand what questions are invasive, Mari provides this opportunity for learning so mistakes aren't made in the future. They say, "I love answering those questions because I want to help people understand and I also want to help people redirect their inappropriate, possibly offensive, questions to me, who is sitting in the educator space, rather than the people that are just in this person's life. I would much rather have them come to an actual educator than just a trans person or an intersex person that's existing."

OUT TEACHERS

Given the impact of the Lavender Scare in the 1950s and the societal messages degrading queer teachers, it was and continues to be a powerful statement for a teacher to be openly LGBTQ. Messages about gay and trans people being "predators" or "groomers" has long been a technique to stigmatize queer people and distract from other political issues of the time, namely sexual abuse or violence perpetrated by non-LGBTQ people. One historic example is the investigations of Florida teachers in the 1950s. It is estimated that over one hundred teachers lost their jobs in Florida in 1956 due to anti-gay policies, which makes the anti-LGBTQ education policies vilifying affirming educators and removing inclusive curriculum and books even more chilling and reminiscent of this history.

Only twenty states, as well as Puerto Rico and DC, have state laws that prohibit discrimination in schools on the basis of sexual orientation and gender identity. Being an out teacher can come with risks—and also rewards, as it is incredibly meaningful for LGBTQ+ young people to see themselves reflected in their school's faculty. Teachers can find community with one another through faculty affinity groups, or national resources can help them find support and know they're not alone. In 1974, the first association for LGBTQ teachers was created in New York, called the Gay Teachers Association, and many more have emerged since then, like the virtual Queer Teachers Rock! support group from Queer Kids Stuff.

BUILDING THE MOVEMENT

From the 1970s to the 1990s, a growing number of GSAs and youth-led action led to a need for resources and a national strategy. Groups like the GSA Network, GLSEN, and PFLAG emerged to provide national support to GSAs, as well as to schools and families. With the support of the national organizations, events like National Coming Out Day (originated in 1988; annually on Oct. 11), LGBT History Month (originated in 1994), and the Day of Silence (originated in 1996) became tangible opportunities for entire school communities to recognize LGBTQ people. Every two years, GLSEN also publishes the National School Climate Survey, which collects experiences from LGBTQ+ students in schools about a range of issues from bullying to inclusive curriculum to bathroom access and much more. These large-scale national initiatives offer a collective resource for schools all across the country to organize around particular issues.

What can schools and the education system do to best support all students? If you're in school now, how does your school specifically address LGBTQ+ inclusion and education? What are you involved with as a student?

Advances in Education

1970: Bob Martin and other students found the first gay student organization in the country at Columbia University. First called The Student Homophile League, the group later becomes Gay People at Columbia-Barnard, focused on activism and social dances. They formed a gay lounge in 1971; it is now known as the Stephen Donaldson Queer Lounge.

1972: Youth at the NYC George Washington High School found the first secondary-school-based gay group on record in the United States.

1973: Jeanne Manford founds Parents, Families, and Friends of Lesbians and Gays (PFLAG) to provide support to other parents. Jeanne was an elementary school teacher and parent to Morty Manford, who participated in the Stonewall Inn riots of 1969. She made history when she became the first parent to publicly march in solidarity and support of LGBTQ+ rights. In 2012, she received the Presidential Citizens Medal.

1984: Dr. Virginia Uribe, a science teacher and college counselor at Fairfax High School in Los Angeles, California, founds Project 10. Dr. Uribe was one of the first educators in the Los Angeles Unified School District to come out. This group inspired Project 10 East at the Cambridge Rindge and Latin School in Cambridge, Massachusetts, as well as many GSAs to follow.

1984: The Federal Equal Access Act is passed and gives fair opportunity to students who want to create meetings or clubs. If even one non-curricular club is allowed, schools must allow other clubs and cannot discriminate on the basis of that club's purpose or discussions. This means that GSAs (Gender-Sexuality Alliances or Gay-Straight Alliances) are protected nationally under the law. Kelli Peterson, a student at East High School in Salt Lake City, Utah, founds a GSA at her school in 1996, followed by her school board banning all non-curricular clubs in order to prevent the GSA from forming. She becomes the subject of *Out of the Past*, a documentary.

1985:   New York's Harvey Milk High School becomes the first public high school in the country for youth harmed by homophobia and transphobia. The school was named after Harvey Milk (1930–1978), who was one of the first openly gay elected officials in the United States.

1994:   Rodney Wilson, an openly gay high school teacher in Missouri, creates Lesbian and Gay History Month (Transgender, Bisexual, and Queer are added later). The National Education Association passes a resolution in support in 1995. LGBTQ+ History Month continues to be celebrated every October, which is a significant month that contains National Coming Out Day and the anniversaries of the 1979 and 1987 Marches on Washington for Lesbian and Gay Rights.

1996:   The first Day of Silence is organized as a protest by students at the University of Virginia with 150 students participating. This annual day of action against bullying and harassment is now hosted by GLSEN and honored at schools across the country every April.

1998:   The GSA Network is founded as a national youth-driven organization in San Francisco to connect LGBTQ+ youth and school-based GSA clubs with peer support, leadership development, and community organizing and advocacy. They create the National Association of GSA Networks in 2005 to grow the national movement. Their resources and programming prioritize youth organizing at the intersection of racial and gender justice.

2011:   Trans Student Educational Resources (TSER) becomes the only national organization led entirely by trans youth. It is dedicated to transforming educational spaces for trans and gender nonconforming students.

2018:   National Deaf LGBTQ Awareness Week begins and is recognized in schools across the country. This annual educational week is led by the Deaf Queer Resource Center (DQRC), which was founded by Dragonsani "Drago" Renteria, a Deaf Chicano trans and queer activist. Drago also publishes *CTN Magazine*, the first national magazine for the Deaf queer community, while running the Deaf Gay and Lesbian Center in San Francisco.

2019:   The organization Asexual Awareness begins leading Ace Week, formerly Asexual Awareness Week, founded by Sara Beth Brooks in 2010. Ace Week is "an international campaign dedicated to raising awareness and expanding education of asexuality." It provides resources and educational materials to community organizers.

"The lack of representation of the LGBTQIA+ community is a universal issue. However, my identity tends to be the least represented and most often overlooked. A part of my sexuality is being asexual, a term I recently discovered in the last year or so. Asexuality is never mentioned in sex ed, which makes teens who feel this way even more confused and feel more isolated. Asexuality is so complex and such an isolating discovery that without the proper representation and conversations, it can lead to the mentality of 'something is wrong with me,' when it's just how you are born and slowly discovering."
—Faith Cardillo, activist (chapter 4)

FAITH CARDILLO

2023: GLSEN's Rise Up Resolution is introduced in Congress with the support of Senator Brian Schatz, Representative Mark Takano, and Representative Barbara Lee. The resolution calls for equal education opportunity, basic civil rights protections, and freedom from erasure for students. On their webpage, GLSEN released a pledge:

1. I pledge to advocate for safe learning environments where young people, their teachers, and school staff are free from the violence of racism, transphobia, homophobia, sexism, ableism, and all forms of systemic oppression.
2. I pledge to advocate for LGBTQ+ affirming books, resources, and curriculum in schools.
3. I pledge to rise up against hateful anti-LGBTQ+ bills and rhetoric.

"I was able to realize that I was gonna be all right, and that the work I was doing moving forward wasn't for myself, but for the other Ashtons out there who didn't have that initial support, or who are still navigating their identity." —Ashton Mota

ASHTON MOTA
(HE/HIM)

Ashton Mota is a Black Afro-Latino advocate for change driven to achieve justice, equity, and equality for all. He says, "Living my life authentically, and being proud of that, and doing advocacy in that way, and showing the world that I'm a young trans person who's thriving, I think that's advocacy within itself."

Ashton grew up in Lowell, Massachusetts, where his first major experience with advocacy work started with the Yes on 3 campaign in 2018. Massachusetts proposed a ballot question that would determine whether transgender people would continue to be protected in accessing public spaces. At the time, Ashton was fourteen years old, and he says this advocacy opportunity solidified for him the importance of having young LGBTQ+ people lead. Ashton says, "Our stories and our experiences were the ones that a lot of the public who didn't really have a direct connection to transgender people resonated with, and that was because when they saw us speak, and they saw young people be so passionate about these topics, it kind of made it simpler."

Alongside a team of youth volunteers and his mom, Ashton made phone calls, knocked on doors, and spoke at larger gatherings to help people in Massachusetts understand the importance of protecting trans rights. He helped humanize this ballot question by talking directly with people. He says, "I remember a lot of my remarks had to do with, you know, I'm just a kid, and I want to be able to go to the movie theater, use the bathroom, and be out in public with my friends on the weekend without having to worry about my safety. And I think kind of giving that perspective to a lot of people changed their view on it. I feel like actually getting

to meet transgender young people and see that they weren't the people that were being portrayed in the media was definitely an experience for people to be able to see for example, their own child in us, or their nephew, or their neighbor in us."

Ashton and his family do a lot of work at the national level too. Two of Ashton's siblings are part of the foster care system, and they both happen to be trans women of color. His family has met with the Secretary of Health and Human Services to address flaws in the education and foster care systems that his family has experienced firsthand. In 2021, Ashton introduced President Biden at the White House's Pride Month celebration, the first to happen in four years. Leading up to the Pride celebration, Ashton met with Ambassador Susan Rice alongside three other transgender youth activists to voice the needs of trans students. That same year, Ashton coauthored his first book. Through his work with the GenderCool Project, Ashton and Rebekah Bruesehoff wrote *A Kids Book about Being Inclusive*, which empowers young people with the tools to be inclusive.

Ashton is most proud of recently spending his junior year abroad in Spain, which gave him a fuller, more global perspective on his activism. He says, "I was able to take away from the experience not only just learning the Spanish language, but the culture, and the experience of being a young person living away from home. It changed me as a person, and I've also seen how those changes have applied to my day-to-day life here in the US, specifically when it comes to activism and advocacy work. I feel like I have a more global lens on things." Ashton loves being surrounded by his family and friends, listening to music or podcasts, and is excited to start learning the guitar.

"I didn't wake up one day and decide to
become involved in education and liberation
work; it was a matter of survival."
—Blair Imani

BLAIR IMANI
(SHE/HER)

Blair Imani is a Black bisexual Muslim educator whose main goal is to help people become just a little smarter or more informed one post, discussion, video, or product at a time. Through her viral web series *Smarter in Seconds* and her writing, Blair shares accessible education focused on history, sociology, and anti-oppression education in collaboration with other creators like Schuyler Bailar, Addison Rose Vincent, and Kahlil Greene. Blair helps people seek, vet, and cite credible sources as a way of countering harmful misinformation on the internet. She's written three books: *Modern Herstory*, *Making Our Way Home*, and *Read This to Get Smarter*.

Like many people doing this work, Blair's motivation started from a place of survival. She says, "In college at Louisiana State University, I felt that if I didn't reschedule my classes to make time to go to the Louisiana State Legislature on a regular basis, I was being irresponsible and negligent to the suffering of my LGBTQ+ peers, friends, and community members who were being forced into conversion therapy, denied housing, and denied jobs. I didn't approach my early student organizing days in the healthiest way. I should've spent more time taking breaks, incorporating balance, and taking the time to surround myself with people who would support me regardless of how 'useful' I was to them. At that time, I learned just how much youth LGBTQ+ organizers can learn from our LGBTQ+ elders."

Mentors and elders made a huge difference. She says, "I met a transgender lesbian couple who were both Vietnam War veterans. They were working in New Orleans while I was based out in Baton Rouge, and over time they helped me to view the fight for LGBTQ+ liberation as a marathon instead of a sprint. It took some time for me to fully embrace that message, but I am so grateful that they took the time to impart that wisdom to me and show me that young people are not the only ones with something to offer."

Blair loves lipstick and is proud of her partnership with her friends Dr. Christina Basias and Alexis Androulakis, the married cofounders of Fempower Beauty, who launched Blair's signature lipstick. They brainstormed ways to incorporate education through the medium of beauty while also healing the harms of the beauty industry with an array of products and services that affirm and uplift. She says, "Every lipstick in the Smarter Lip Sets collection that we created together comes with a Smarter in Seconds lesson that corresponds to a chapter in *Read This to Get Smarter*. I am just so proud to be doing this work with my friends with an innovative, pro-LGBTQ, pro-human, ethical approach with high-quality products to match. I am living my wildest dreams—even dreams I never thought could be remotely realistic—and that is the thing I'm most proud of."

Blair finds much joy in traveling, trying new foods, watching very long YouTube videos about obscure topics, and going to see movies. She plans to pursue her dreams of producing television—in the footsteps of people like Issa Rae and Quinta Brunson—and has her first executive producer credit to celebrate. Looking ahead, she says, "I hope that in the future I am able to enjoy even more opportunities and include as many people as possible in the work that I continue to create."

"There are more LGBTQ activists now than, I believe, ever. And I think
that our generation, or young people in general, is going to pave the way
for more rights, and more of the basic treatments that LGBTQ people
don't get. We definitely should thank the people at Stonewall especially,
like Marsha P. Johnson. In the future, I just hope that we can do more to
support LGBTQ youth, and anyone who is queer, because it's still not safe
to be LGBTQ, especially for youth who live in small towns." —Desi Napoles

DESMOND (DESI) NAPOLES
(THEY/THEM)

Desmond (Desi) Napoles is an educator, activist, and performer who is envisioning a world where all queer and nonbinary youth can be their full selves. Desi's motto is "Be yourself, always." Desi started their activism as a drag kid expressing themself through makeup and fashion to inspire other youth to explore their creativity too. They reach young people through public performances and speeches, social media, writing, and news articles. While they still admire and support the art of drag performance, they no longer describe themselves as a drag performer. When it comes to their own gender identity, they say, "I wouldn't call it drag. I would call it me being me. I'm not putting on a character, I'm just being me. Drag just didn't fit my label anymore after I found out that I was nonbinary."

Whitewashing is when the telling of history or the honor of accolades favors white people or puts white people's achievements above others. Think of the ways Florida legislators have attempted to remove Black studies from the state's curriculum or ban books by Black authors, or the fact that only eleven Black artists have won album of the year in the Grammy Awards' 66-year history. The accolades are not a true reflection of who is "best" or most accomplished, or whose history deserves to be told, but rather a reflection of the storyteller or decision-maker's bias toward white people and white-centered narratives.

At events like Drag Queen Story Hour, Desi educates youth and families in their community about LGBTQ history and how we got the rights we deserve today. Their book, *Be Amazing: A History of Pride*, highlights three iconic LGBTQ people: Marsha P. Johnson, Sylvia Rivera, and RuPaul. Desi wrote this book so youth could see themselves and their histories represented. Desi wanted youth to feel the way they did when they learned about Sylvia Rivera's activism. Desi immediately related to Sylvia Rivera's story, as they are both Puerto Rican trans activists, and this inspired them to educate other youth about Sylvia Rivera's impact on our community.

Desi says, "[Learning about Sylvia] really changed my perspective on race in the LGBTQ community, and how a lot of LGBTQ history has been whitewashed, so I really think that changed my perspective on sharing these histories." Desi hopes that more people will learn about the legacies of Black and Latine people who paved the way for LGBTQ liberation, and wants to see more LGBTQ history taught in schools.

In 2022, when hundreds of anti-LGBTQ bills were being proposed, Desi spoke on their Instagram live about the bills and their impact on LGBTQ youth. Alongside educating people on Instagram, they participate in meetings at the New York City ACLU Teen Activist Project to address issues affecting LGBTQ youth in schools. Desi is working with the ACLU to propose better policies and legislation that will support LGBTQ youth to counteract and challenge the harmful legislation happening all across the country. Desi became an advisory member of the Born This Way Foundation in 2023 to "advise on their mission of supporting youth mental health and building a kinder and braver world."

Desi is grateful to have a family that supports all of their activism efforts. They say, "I have an accepting family. I wish that more LGBTQ people had accepting families like mine. I think that is really unfortunate and I hope that can change over time, because queer people shouldn't have to worry about being kicked out of their house for being who they are. And I just really want to thank my family for supporting me." Through events like Drag Queen Story Hour and speaking publicly at other events, Desi helps open the hearts and minds of families so they can better support their LGBTQ children.

One thing that brings Desi a lot of joy and curiosity outside activism is subway trains. They love learning about the history of trains and how they're built, and they even build railway lines of their own through video games like *NIMBY Rails* on Steam. They say, "It makes me really happy to express my creativity on there and build train lines onto a real-world map." Desi hopes to drive subway trains for the MTA someday.

DRAG STORY HOUR

Drag story hours are fun events for children that celebrate reading, self-expression, and acceptance. Credited to author and activist Michelle Tea from San Francisco beginning in 2015, the movement is focused on bringing inclusive books to children. Common titles include *When Aidan Became a Brother* by Kyle Lukoff; *Red: A Crayon's Story* by Michael Hall; *The Family Book* by Todd Parr; and *Julian Is a Mermaid* by Jessica Love, among many others. Unfortunately, in recent years drag story hours have been targeted by legislation that would criminalize these events and they've seen anti-LGBTQIA+ protesters at the events themselves. Volunteer-led efforts around the country, like the Parasol Patrol, shield young people from the protesters with colorful rainbow umbrellas and positive messages allowing youth and families to peacefully arrive and enjoy their events.

"Young people are the core center front of liberation. Obviously that comes from people of color. I believe that if we're going to be creating anything for youth, that we should be involving youth, right? They should be directly taking part in the work that we're doing. I see a lot of people trying to create things for youth and they're not even talking to youth. They don't know what our needs or demands are." —JP Grant

JP GRANT
(HE/HIM)

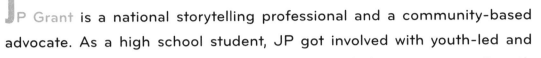

JP Grant is a national storytelling professional and a community-based advocate. As a high school student, JP got involved with youth-led and -centered organizations like Project 351, a movement of youth leaders in Massachusetts, and GLSEN's National Student Council. JP says that these opportunities were a catalyst for his growth and introduced him to other youth leaders passionate about education and advocacy.

JP later worked as a health educator in Boston's public schools, where he saw "a lot of need for personal development and leadership skills" among the students he worked with. As an educator, JP uplifts social emotional learning, sex education, intersectionality, and resources for neurodivergent students like him. Through the Getting to Zero Activist Academy at Fenway Health, JP created resources for people in Massachusetts to advocate for the Healthy Youth Act, a bill that would require comprehensive, consent-based, LGBTQ-inclusive, medically accurate sexual health education. In July 2022, JP spoke at a rally at the State House to demand the passage of this critical piece of legislation.

Just weeks before the rally, JP released his debut book, *Refine Your Most Successful Narrative: Turn Your Dreams to Reality*, and launched his business. Refine Your Narrative LLC helps medical professionals and professional educators become champions in the workplace by creating dialogue. Their vision is that "conversations begin when shaming ends." JP says, "We must build a platform, especially for QTBIPOC communities. As someone who is queer, someone who is Black and someone who's Latine, I thought that there was a way for me to alleviate the painful process of

having to find resources or having to find a sense of community or empowerment, and so I wanted to uplift other people."

JP also wants people to understand that he didn't magically arrive where he's at today—he faced many challenges as a young person and had to find support. He says during his interview, "The fact that I had consecutive years of mental health treatment is something that I've never really shared, and that I've been homeless is something that I've never shared. It was me literally being in the dark that showed me there's so many ways to get out of here and that's when I started to actually put in the work. People will ask, 'What are your credentials?' and of course I could list them for you, but I'll tell them straight up it's the tears, blood, and sweat that is my PhD. My faith is so much greater than my fear, and that is what has gotten me here today." Now, his work mainly involves helping mission-driven CEOs become storytellers so they can build their businesses without imposter syndrome.

HEALTHY YOUTH ACT

If the Healthy Youth Act passes, public schools in Massachusetts that do teach sex ed would have to choose a curriculum that aligns with the standards set forth in the act. Other states, like Illinois, have gone through the process of passing bills similar to the Healthy Youth Act in order to update their curricula.

JP finds joy in listening to podcasts and is planning a podcast with his friend about empowerment for BIPOC communities. He says he's an old soul who enjoys being out in nature, hanging out with friends and family, reading, and writing. His work requires a lot of emotional labor, so he takes great pride in taking care of his physical, social, and mental health. It's also a way of modeling for others what he hopes they'll be able to achieve for themselves. He says, "We deserve to be heard, and we deserve to leverage our power."

"I will *never* be able to leave my Blackness at home. I will *never* be able to leave my queerness at home. As a Black, Latine, and QUEER business owner, I had to build a platform for folks to alleviate the pain process of looking for resources for their basic needs. We deserve equitable health care and justice just like everyone else."

—JP Grant, speech at a rally for inclusive sexual health education in Boston, July 2022

"Don't let any moment of adversity or despair derail you from your purpose. Each and every one of us deserves a life of peace, joy, and happiness, whatever that looks like for you."
—Mallery Jenna Robinson

MALLERY JENNA ROBINSON
(SHE/HER)

Mallery Jenna Robinson is an AfraCaribbean transgender activist and HIV health care advocate who previously taught middle school in Florida. "I still feel like I'm always teaching the community, accomplices, and allies about our community and our needs. I'm not directly in a classroom anymore, but I still feel like that education piece is there," she says.

In August 2022, Mallery curated an exhibit for Long Beach Pride in Long Beach, California, highlighting Marsha P. Johnson and other trancestors dating all the way back to the 1800s. The pop-up museum was called Transcendence Dome. Mallery says, "You were able to walk in and see all of the sheroes and their stories, and the heroes too, transmasculine folks." Opening day began with a ribbon-cutting ceremony alongside the TransLatin@ Coalition, a grassroots organization founded in 2009 by a group of trans-gender, gender nonconforming, and intersex (TGI) immigrant women in Los Angeles, California.

Though Mallery didn't begin doing advocacy work pro-fessionally until 2018, she says that it truly began for her as early as 2006, when she was sixteen and started authentically showing up as herself every day. She has very supportive family and friends who cele-brate her, including her high school classmates. She says, "I went to prom as female-presenting. I took my senior pictures as female-presenting. I was determined, even in high school, to not let anyone police my gender jour-ney, my gender identity, or my gender period."

In 2021, Mallery began recording and releasing *A Hateful Homicide*, a true-crime and investigative journalism podcast focused on the murders of transgender, gender nonbinary/non-conforming, intersex, Two-Spirit, and gender expansive community members throughout the United States, including Rita Hester, a Black trans woman from Boston whose death sparked the Transgender Day of Remembrance movement; Tony McDade, a Black trans man killed by police in Tallahassee, Florida, in 2020; and many others. Mallery is passionate about highlighting the voices of people whose lives were taken by police brutality, transphobia, and intimate partner violence.

Looking ahead, Mallery looks forward to continuing her work in the entertainment industry. She says, "I feel that there's still not enough

SAY THEIR NAMES

To uplift the Black Lives Matter movement at a major university, Felicia A. Smith, an African American librarian, created the *Say Their Names—No More Names* exhibit at Stanford University. The exhibit honors 330 people, with 65 stories featured, including transgender people Tony McDade, Nina Pop, and Dominique Fells. It also documents systemic racism, including the Chicago Police torture victims, the Black Wall Street Massacre, and the Tuskegee Syphilis Experiment. Smith successfully advocated for the libraries at Stanford to be closed in observance of Juneteenth, now a national holiday that commemorates the emancipation of enslaved African Americans. Smith and the wider Black Lives Matter movement call for "No more names!": no more murders of Black people at the hands of police brutality and systemic violence.

representation until there's accessibility, visibility, and equity for each and every one of us in every venue. There's still a lot of work to be done." Mallery remembers growing up watching *America's Next Top Model* and seeing Isis King, the first trans woman to compete on the show. Beyond that, she didn't see much representation and wants to continue changing that. She says, "Black trans women are worthy of being on *The Bachelorette*. We're worthy of being on daytime soap operas if we want to. We're worthy of just appearing in whatever we want to pursue, whether that's playing a trans role or a cis role or a nonbinary role."

When she isn't auditioning at casting calls, Mallery is also in the studio recording music. Mallery finds joy in spending time with her chosen family. "I've developed this incredible chosen family of queer and trans people of color," she says. They all love going hiking together, hanging out at the beach, and hosting parties to celebrate one another. Mallery hosted a chosen family Christmas party one year to create connections for those who may not have supportive families and can't visit home. She says, "I love to be able to provide this space as a safe space for the community. They'll come over to my apartment and we'll do game nights. Seeing my community have a space to come and have joy and feel safe—the laughter, all of that just brings me joy."

"By having young people in education and advocacy, we're essentially telling other young people that they have a story worth listening to. And that they deserve to be heard, and that is why I do so much of what I do."
—Mari Wrobi

MARI WROBI
(THEY/THEM)

In the winter of 2019, at the annual Creating Change conference in Detroit, Mari spoke publicly for the first time about intersex advocacy. "This was my first time doing any kind of intersex advocacy work, as I was just starting to come into the realization that I was intersex myself, and that I had this whole community. Because I'm a natural educator, that's where my passions lie, and I thought, 'I want to turn this experience into something that can help more people,'" Mari reflects. After the presentation, Mari got a message from interACT, an organization that empowers young intersex advocates and promotes laws protecting intersex youth. Hans Lindahl, now an intersex educator focused on training medical schools, provided mentorship to Mari that jumpstarted their activist work alongside other intersex youth organizers.

Mari's path toward education and advocacy started long before their presentation at Creating Change, though. "When I first entered the LGBTQ community, I was twelve or thirteen. I remember at the time, first of all, feeling a little disconnected from advocacy work in general. I had opportunities, but the advocacy work that existed at the time felt very limited. I didn't feel like I had a voice that anyone wanted to listen to." As the only out trans person at their high school, Mari had to quickly learn self-advocacy and how to connect with supportive teachers. Mari remembers looking to well-spoken adult advocates with compelling stories and worrying that their own story wasn't enough as a young advocate. That changed when they saw other young people using their voices to advocate for the rights of others. Now, they say, "I want intersex people to feel like they have a voice and like they are being heard and listened to and recognized because so many intersex people are the ones experiencing the harshest discrimination and prejudices."

Mari lives in Sacramento, the capital of California, where they first connected with interACT organizers and had the opportunity to share their story at the Capitol. "I don't care if it's every single year that I have to go down to the Capitol. I'll do it, and I'm excited to because I want to finally have a state in the US that delays non-consensual surgeries on intersex youth." They've learned a lot about the process of policy advocacy and lobbying through their work with three organizations—interACT, InterConnect, and the Intersex Justice Project. Looking to intersex advocates before them, Mari appreciates the leadership of people like Sean Saifa Wall and Pidgeon Pagonis, cofounders of the Intersex Justice Project, and Bria Brown-King, the engagement director at interACT: Advocates for Intersex Youth.

By providing educational workshops across the country and creating social media content on TikTok and Instagram, Mari is sharing their voice as a Latinx Mexican queer, nonbinary, trans, and intersex person, educator,

"IT'S ALSO IMPORTANT TO RECOGNIZE THAT MANY OF THE GENITAL SURGERIES THAT BECAME AVAILABLE TO LATER GENERATIONS OF TRANSGENDER PEOPLE WERE DEVELOPED BY PRACTICING ON THE BODIES OF ENSLAVED BLACK WOMEN WHO WERE SUBJECTED TO MEDICAL EXPERIMENTATION, AND THAT THESE PROCEDURES WERE USED NONCONSENSUALLY ON THE BODIES OF INTERSEX YOUTH."

—SUSAN STRYKER, *TRANSGENDER HISTORY*

INTERSEX ADVOCACY

We've often been taught not only a strict gender binary, but a binary related to biology, which is simply not scientifically true. There are many people who are born intersex, which according to interACT is "an umbrella term for unique variations in reproductive or sex anatomy. Variations may appear in a person's chromosomes, genitals, or internal organs like testes or ovaries. Some intersex traits are identified at birth, while others may not be discovered until puberty or later in life." Intersex advocates are calling for an end to nonconsensual surgeries in infancy. Several national medical associations (American Academy of Family Physicians; GLMA: Health Professionals Advancing LGBTQ+ Equality; and the American Counseling Association) and two state medical associations (Massachusetts and Michigan) have proclaimed that intersex people should have autonomy over decisions about their bodies. Intersex activists ask for solidarity from the larger LGBTQ+ community to support their advocacy work, given the long history of marginalization and violence toward intersex individuals and communities.

and advocate. They are creating the resources they wish they had as a young person. They understand that most people haven't learned about intersex history, so they're creating educational content on TikTok to highlight people like Thomas(ine) Hall, one of the most well-documented intersex people in history; or the story of the intersex flag created by Morgan Carpenter in 2013.

Outside advocacy, Mari loves exploring their creative, nerdy personality. "Writing has been a huge source of comfort for me, like journaling, poetry, spoken word." They realized that writing is an outlet where they can explore their intersex experience, focusing on their own feelings and thoughts, without needing to educate or advocate. It's a creative outlet that is just for them. Mari also finds joy in creating colorful art and hosting Dungeons & Dragons and Magic: The Gathering game nights.

"We're building on the foundations that the activists
before us built. They've been doing this for decades
and because of how much progress they've made,
I'm able to live my life and thrive as me."
—Rebekah Bruesehoff

REBEKAH BRUESEHOFF
(SHE/HER)

Rebekah Bruesehoff is an activist, advocate, author, and nerd who loves reading and playing field hockey with her supportive teammates. She first gained public attention when a photo from a rally for trans students went viral. With pink hair and a big smile, she held a sign reading, "I'm the scary transgender person the media warned you about." She is dedicated to uplifting and normalizing the stories of joyful trans kids like herself. Rebekah is especially proud of writing her first book. In 2021, she coauthored *A Kids Book about Being Inclusive* with Ashton Mota as part of a series for the GenderCool Project. She says, "My favorite part about that project had to be that it was unique because it took these big topics and put them into words that kids could understand, that they were meant to understand. It really shows that they're ready for big ideas, they're ready and they're capable of learning. And when we're able to teach young kids about inclusion, that's how we make a better world."

Both Ashton and Rebekah are GenderCool Champions who speak and write on behalf of the GenderCool Project, a national youth-led story-telling organization. Through GenderCool, Rebekah was a reverse mentor (a young person mentoring an adult) for a STEM company, teaching them how to make their space more inclusive for the next generation of leaders in technology. She loves speaking to groups about inclusivity because it's "all about who we are and not just what the world thinks we are." She doesn't want to be defined just by her trans identity, and wants all trans youth to be understood as full people. She says, "People tell me that I'm brave for being myself, but I don't want to have to be brave. I just want it to

be seen as someone being themselves. It shouldn't be that hard to be able to create a world where that is the case."

Rebekah is grateful to have a supportive family who she says were "crucial in my transition and making me the happy person that I am right now." Her faith is an important part of her identity, so she's passionate about "speaking out about how being LGBTQ and Christian aren't mutually exclusive." In 2018, she spoke alongside her mom at the Evangelical Lutheran Church in America (ELCA) Youth Gathering in Houston, Texas, to 31,000 youth and adults. Rebekah was the first openly transgender person to speak at an ELCA Youth Gathering. She encouraged everyone there to listen to the voices of young people and to promote inclusion.

In 2019, the Mighty Rebekah joined the Marvel Universe as their newest superhero. The Marvel Hero Project features young people who are purposeful leaders in their communities. Rebekah has been a model for kind, thoughtful change-making in her advocacy work, and this was yet another way for Rebekah and her family to share their story of love and joy.

In addition to her family, Rebekah has many heroes in her own life, including her peers at GenderCool, as well as trans advocates like Raquel Willis, author and media strategist, and Sarah McBride, Delaware state senator. She believes that all trans kids are truly superheroes and sees a future where we are all celebrated for who we are. She uses her voice for change by working with the Congressional Equality Caucus to defeat trans athlete bans, testifying at the New Jersey State House to protect libraries from book bans, hosting book drives that are LGBTQ+ inclusive, and raising visibility and awareness through media.

Looking ahead, Rebekah is simply hoping to "make a positive impact on the world." She's also excited about writing another book soon, which will hopefully be a creative memoir highlighting everything she's learned about advocacy in her life. In the meantime, she is spending time laughing with her friends, exploring the outdoors, and finding peace in nature.

"Looking back on myself at fourteen, I'm just so proud of who I was. I'm so proud of how much I've grown and I hope that I continue to grow and evolve in my ideas, my views, and the things that I want for myself."
—Sameer Hussain Jha

SAMEER HUSSAIN JHA
(ANY PRONOUNS)

Sameer Hussain Jha is a queer, nonbinary South Asian educator and artist. They grew up in Fremont, California, where their early experiences of being bullied as a queer student motivated them to become an "educator of the educators." At fourteen years old, Sameer founded the Empathy Alliance, a national organization that continues to make schools safer and more inclusive for LGBTQ+ youth.

After finding supportive adults and friends in high school, Sameer wanted to create more spaces where other LGBTQ youth could be their authentic selves too. He says, "I was always gender nonconforming. I love musical theater and the color pink. I was bullied all throughout elementary and middle school. That only really changed when I went to a different school in Oakland that was really diverse. It had openly queer students and faculty, and the GSA club was the largest club on campus. That was where I was able to really come to terms with being queer and nonbinary because I was able to see that, you know, 'gay' wasn't an insult. That it was something that people identified with and were proud of."

Seeing this model of inclusivity gave Sameer the confidence to return to his middle school as an older student to advocate for change and train their former teachers. In 2016, she met with the counselor and principal there, who were receptive to making changes within the school, like starting the first GSA in the school's history. To Sameer's surprise, they needed overflow space for the first meeting because Sameer says there were "so many people that felt the way I did." Soon after, Sameer advocated for inclusive sexual health education in the Fremont Unified School District

and hosted events in Fremont to raise awareness in the South Asian community, like Chai with Sameer, an open discussion for South Asian people to share their experiences and connect with each other. In 2018, they helped host the first-ever Fremont Pride celebration that was cosponsored with the city.

This is how the Empathy Alliance was born and soon grew into meaningful workshops that have reached over one million educators and students. Sameer finds joy and healing in facilitating these spaces. She says, "I've always loved teaching, ever since I was a little kid. A lot of my activism is centered around teachers and the school system and the school environment, and my job is to educate the educators." In 2018, they captured their story and the lessons of these workshops in their first book, *Read This, Save Lives: A Teacher's Guide to Creating Safer Classrooms for LGBTQ+ Students*.

While launching the Empathy Alliance, Sameer worked with other youth-led and -centered programs like the GSA Network, the Human Rights Campaign Foundation's Youth Ambassador program, and the GLSEN National Student Council. He says that "being able to be a part of these groups of LGBTQ+ youth that are all trying to make a change and to fight for the difference that we want to see—I think that experience of bonding is so incredible because sometimes it is really isolating, especially for me, where I was one of the only out people doing the work in my community."

For Pride Month in 2021, Sameer was invited to the White House by President Biden to mark the passing of a bill that made Pulse Nightclub a national memorial. A few months later, Sameer provided policy recommendations to four US federal departments about the needs of trans youth in schools. The Empathy Alliance has led Sameer to national platforms that create tangible changes for LGBTQ+ youth, like partnering with GLSEN in 2018 for a national campaign supporting GSAs. In addition to continuing this important work, she plans to become a teacher because "educators and schools can change the lives of LGBTQ+ students, and for me this was absolutely true. Seeing out, supportive queer faculty and teachers was absolutely life changing for me. I would love to be that source of support for students."

Ever since they were very young, Sameer has loved performing musical theater. In elementary and middle school, they performed in at least three musicals a year. It brings her so much joy to sing and express herself. As a student at Stanford University, Sameer is working on initiatives to make theater more representative and inclusive. He's also creating queer pop music under the name Sami Hussain as another way of expressing the things that matter to him most as a queer South Asian activist.

PULSE NIGHTCLUB

On June 12, 2016, forty-nine people were killed and fifty-three injured in a mass shooting at the gay nightclub Pulse, in Orlando, Florida. In 2019, the **onePULSE Foundation** was established to honor the lives taken by gun violence and to honor their legacies by awarding annual higher learning scholarships to forty-nine people based on each of the victims' interests, careers, or aspirations. Marking **Pulse Nightclub** as a national memorial site held a great deal of significance for the many friends, family, and survivors of the Pulse Nightclub Massacre, as well as the wider community.

"My parents were always my role models. I never looked up to celebrities, partially because of representation. There weren't other queer, trans, half-Korean athletes out there that I knew of, and even now I struggle to find others who can mirror all of my identities." —Schuyler Bailar

SCHUYLER BAILAR
(HE/HIM)

When Schuyler Bailar came out on Facebook as a transgender man at the age of nineteen, he blocked his grandmother from seeing the post. He was worried that his grandparents would judge him or not understand who he was. He wrote a letter and read it to them instead. His grandmother said, "Okay, that's fine. Now I have two grandsons from your mother." Schuyler underestimated the love and acceptance he'd receive from his grandparents and, later, his community at Harvard University.

Schuyler grew up in Virginia, where he and his brother began swimming as soon as they could. In high school, he set records for swimming and was on several national championship teams. In 2013, Schuyler was recruited by Harvard University's women's swim team. There was a lot going on for Schuyler at the time, but he was certain about one thing—he wanted to swim no matter what. If he wanted to be successful on the Harvard swim team, he needed to take care of himself first. Schuyler was struggling with an eating disorder and decided to take a gap year after graduating high school to enroll in a residential treatment center for eating disorders. This is also where he first met other transgender youth and began finding the words to describe his own experiences.

Schuyler finished treatment for his mental health and went on to pursue medical care for his transition. Schuyler had a choice to make: Would he swim on the women's team or the men's team? He had frequent meetings with the coaches at Harvard during his treatment and began confiding in them about his gender. To his surprise, the coach of the men's team and all his soon-to-be teammates welcomed Schuyler. He became the first transgender athlete to compete on any NCAA Division I men's team, and, at the time of his graduation, the only one to have competed for all four years. Soon Schuyler was beating his own personal records and graduated college accepting the Harvard Director's Award for his exceptional leadership.

By being his full self and sharing his voice, Schuyler gained a platform to discuss transgender inclusion with schools, workplaces, and universities. Now, he is an internationally celebrated inspirational speaker and educator focused on body acceptance, mental health awareness, and trans rights. You might know Schuyler from his Instagram, @pinkmantaray, where he posts trans-affirming content, advocacy resources, and educational guides. He recognizes that not all young people have accepting families and school communities like he did, or access to medical and mental health care. In 2021, Schuyler released his debut novel, *Obie Is Man Enough*, proclaiming in an Instagram announcement: "This is for all the trans kids out there wondering if you belong. You do. You absolutely do."

His newest book, *He/She/They: How We Talk about Gender and Why It Matters* (2023), is an educational guide capturing Schuyler's years of learning about how to teach others compassionately about gender identity and pronouns. Schuyler says he is proudest of his boldness to "show up every time," and in doing so, he motivates young people around the world to do the same.

"Have people around you who support you. That's something you definitely need. You can think sometimes that you have to do things on your own, but usually that doesn't work. You can't feel scared about asking people to help, because even adults have trouble asking for help." —Trinity Neal

TRINITY NEAL
(SHE/HER)

Trinity Neal is an activist, educator, and lover of coding who speaks about her experiences as a Black transgender girl who is autistic. She is most proud of her first book, *My Rainbow*, coauthored with her mom, DeShanna Neal, which she says teaches people "to be yourself. No matter how hard it is, you can still answer to yourself." The book is a celebration of Trinity's hair, a rainbow wig, which her mom made for her. She says, "My mom decided to make this wig, and that really helped me because in order to feel like you, you have to look like you. That's the only way you can feel like yourself."

Trinity also takes pride in being the first transgender kid to have gained access to puberty blockers in Delaware. Her homeschooling group advocated with her and her mom to change the state's Medicaid requirements so the family could have her medication covered. This activism has allowed other kids like her to get the gender-affirming care they need too. She says about the homeschooling group, "They helped fight with us, and we won because of them. Those people actually helped me grow a lot and showed humanity." When they're not advocating for trans rights, Trinity's home-schooling group also loves playing Dungeons & Dragons together.

Trinity and her mom know how meaningful it is for other trans kids and families to connect with supportive families. They've supported youth in building chosen families and say that "if you have someone who accepts you, they are family." They've spoken about their story in *The Advocate*, *Essence*, *National Geographic*, and *Vice* to create more understanding and education. DeShanna and Trinity's video for Girls Who Code, "On Being," is an illustration of what sisterhood means to them. The vibrant illustrations narrated by DeShanna and Trinity take the viewer on a journey from Trinity's birth, to Trinity expressing that she's a girl at three years old, to the ways

DESHANNA NEAL

Trinity's mom, DeShanna Neal (they/them), is a state representative in Delaware for District 13, advocating for racial justice, accessible medical and mental health care, and LGBTQ+ rights. In 2018, they brought the first-ever drag queen story hour to Delaware. A couple of years later, in 2020, DeShanna founded the Intersections of Pride Foundation focused on supporting LGBTQ and marginalized people in Delaware by providing resources and community outreach.

Trinity and DeShanna practice sisterhood by supporting each other and their community. DeShanna says, "Trinity and I have been a team, which is our version of sisterhood. But I have to say as Trinity's mom, she's my community and my heart, and makes me laugh a lot. And I work hard to be her community and advocate. For us, being a sisterhood means we can now uplift others with our story." Trinity says that, for her, it means "I can share my story of being a happy and thriving Black trans girl."

Trinity says that she's inspired by other trans girls and women who share their stories, too, like writer and director Janet Mock, author and activist Jazz Jennings, and Avery Jackson, who was nine years old when she made history as the first transgender person featured on the cover of *National Geographic*.

There's a lot of joy and color in Trinity's book, which is a perfect reflection of how she describes herself. "I am a person who just likes to have fun and make people feel happy," she says. She also finds joy in playing video games, watching cheesy horror movies, and cleaning her room. Trinity's excited about creating videos for her YouTube channel, where she talks about her favorite games (like *Minecraft* and *Roblox*) and her book. Trinity's advice to you is to "never give up, always have facts, and speak up." Often activists have to carry heavy weights with them. She suggests you turn those heavy weights into positive weights and find joy in everything you do. "Even if no one listens to you, you have to speak up!"

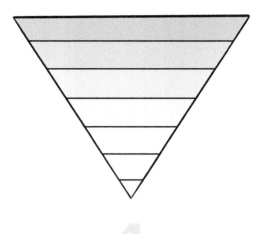

4

FROM WALKOUTS TO MARCHES: DEMANDING QUEER YOUTH SAFETY, AUTONOMY, AND JOY

What are ways that the three types of activists you have read about— organizers, artists, and educators—can come together to share their talents and skills to raise awareness, demand changes from those in power, and make history?

Young people have demonstrated the power of political organizing and protest through walkouts and marches in support of LGBTQ rights, Black Lives Matter, ending gun violence, climate justice, and more. You've read about the Trans Visibility March and the Walkout to Learn (chapter 1) and the Brooklyn Liberation March (chapter 2). One emerging organization, Queer Youth Assemble (QYA), has created youth-led walkouts and marches across the country in the past few years by bringing together all types of young activists in every state.

WHAT IS THE IMPACT OF ANTI-LGBTQ BILLS?

These bills have tangible effects on youth and families, like children of queer parents not being able to talk about their families at school; or parents being criminalized or having their children taken away for accessing lifesaving gender-affirming care; or teachers' classroom libraries being reviewed for any content related to gender, sexuality, and race, leading to fewer resources for students and a culture of fear that may intimidate expert educators. Awareness of these bills alone has severe mental health impacts for LGBTQ youth, according to the Trevor Project.

In the past few years, families have started fleeing states with this legislation to find refuge in safer states. In 2022 sixteen states introduced trans refuge bills, meaning that families could safely move there to get gender-affirming care. The impact of ongoing activism and advocacy by young leaders shifts policy too. By 2024, Florida's "Don't Say Gay" bill remained in place, but a settlement clarified its reach, stating that students and educators could discuss LGBTQ+ topics, as long as those conversations were not part of a formal curriculum. In that same year, a federal judge struck down Florida restrictions on gender-affirming care for both minors and adults, finding them to be unconstitutional.

WALKOUTS

Queer Youth Assemble: "Taking back queer youth autonomy one walkout at a time"

Ten thousand students in twenty-five states walked out of their classrooms on March 11, 2022, to say "We're here, we're queer, and we're not going to live in fear!" Queer Youth Assemble (QYA), an organization led by queer youth for queer youth, called on students across the country to walk out and "take back queer youth autonomy."

In the months leading up to the walkout, hundreds of harmful bills had been introduced across the country that would restrict the rights of trans

"WE MUST HAVE THE AUTONOMY TO CONTROL OUR OWN DESTINIES, BECAUSE ULTIMATELY, ONLY WE KNOW WHAT IS BEST FOR OURSELVES."

—Esmée Silverman

youth to access their education, gender-affirming care, and sports teams. Those that received the most national attention included the "Don't Say Gay" bill in Florida, which prevents educators from discussing LGBTQ+ people and families and which was replicated in multiple states after its passing, and a directive from the Texas governor that criminalizes health care providers and caregivers who provide gender-affirming care to trans youth. Students and families began leading protests in Texas, Florida, and other states where these harmful bills were being proposed. Queer Youth Assemble was inspired by the statewide walkouts

The leadership of Queer Youth Assemble created social media content, like a guide to safely organizing school walkouts. The post spread nationwide, inspiring youth in twenty-five states to prepare walkouts for their schools. Esmée Silverman, QYA cofounder, says, "We were sending out flyers in every single part of the country. We had our network of nationwide QYA volunteers share the graphics to their personal networks. We created webinars to help people who may not necessarily have known exactly how to organize, but were interested in it. We even got celebrities such as ALOK and Chris Mosier to spread the word. Overall the goal was to empower queer youth to create a walkout and as a result we had about ten thousand youth do just that: walk out of their classes to take back their rights."

WALKOUTS

Walkouts have long been a tool of student organizers not only to raise visibility, but also to disrupt school days to make their voices heard and hold the people in power accountable when they've otherwise been silenced or ignored. This organizing strategy has been utilized by the Civil Rights Movement, the Chicano movements of the 1960s and '70s, the climate justice movement, Black Lives Matter, and the gun violence prevention movement, among other movements for justice that impact young people.

In East Los Angeles, around fifteen thousand students walked out of their classrooms in protest March 1–8, 1968. The Educational Issues Coordinating Committee (EICC) voiced the students' concerns during and after the walkout, including presenting a list of demands to the Board of Education in Los Angeles. For decades, disparities for Mexican American students were glaring and harmful. The Chicano movement of the late '60s and early '70s took inspiration from walkouts of the Civil Rights Movement era to stage their own in protest of how Mexican American students were treated by the white minority in their usually majority-Chicano schools, giving preference for sports teams to white students and refusing to include Chicano history in the curriculum. Some students weren't allowed to speak Spanish in school, and the dropout rate for Mexican American students was 60 percent. Chicano students were not receiving full and fair access to education. The demands called for better curriculum, bilingual education, and the hiring of educators who reflected the schools' populations. Though the board denied their demands at the time, the students in East Los Angeles made history by organizing one of the largest student protests in US history. This movement inspired many more walkouts by Chicano students across the Southwest.

Fast forward to March 14, 2018: at 10 a.m. students around the country walked out of their classrooms for the National Student Walkout exactly one month following the school shooting at Marjory Stoneman Douglas High School in Parkland, Florida, calling for gun control. The walkouts lasted at least seventeen minutes, representing the seventeen victims of gun violence. Students called for an end to intersecting forms of oppression, particularly racism, that overlap with gun violence, including police brutality, disproportionate discipline of Black and Brown students, and lack of investment in Black communities.

When Black, queer, and feminist history was being erased from the African American Studies Advanced Placement curriculum in 2023 in Florida, and when Colorado proposed changes to its Advanced Placement History courses that "should not encourage or condone civil disobedience," students walked out to advocate for full access to American history that doesn't censor the realities of oppression in the United States. Across all of these walkouts, students advocated for better education.

in Florida in particular, organized by Jack Petocz from Flagler-Palm Coast High School in early March 2022.

Queer Youth Assemble began in the summer of 2021 when Esmée Silverman and Sawyer Keegan organized Let Trans Athletes Play in Cambridge, Massachusetts. In response to the more than a hundred anti-trans bills being proposed at the time in multiple states, the organizers wanted to create a day not only of protest, but also of joy. They wanted to affirm that trans youth belong everywhere. Let Trans Athletes Play was a day of sports, games, protesting, and action. Eight days later, Esmée Silverman and Cas Rego-Martin founded Queer Youth Assemble, which is "envisioning a world where all queer youth are

SCHUYLER BAILAR

given safety, autonomy, joy, and the ability to reach their fullest potentials." Let Trans Athletes Play has now become an annual event, with Schuyler Bailar joining as the keynote speaker in 2022.

Photo courtesy of Jeremiah Sutherland-Roberts

On March 31, 2022, International Transgender Day of Visibility, the Massachusetts Commission on LGBTQ Youth hosted "We Are a State of Love: A Gathering of Visible Solidarity with LGBTQ Youth" at the State House, just a couple weeks after QYA's first walkout. In response to state-sponsored discrimination in other states across the nation, people gathered on the front steps of the State House to declare: "LGBTQ youth belong here and everywhere!"

Alia Cusolito, QYA co-president, spoke about the impact of youth

Photo courtesy of Michelle Cusolito

organizers and the national QYA walkout alongside legislators, activists, and families. All the founders of QYA are current members or alumni of the GSA Student Leadership Council, a program of the Safe Schools Program for LGBTQ Students. In their speech, Alia honored a council member who died by suicide on March 11, 2020. Queer Youth Assemble chose March 11 as the date for the national walkout to celebrate and mourn their life, and the lives of all youth impacted by anti-LGBTQ violence and stigma.

The walkout in 2022 ignited the next chapter of Queer Youth Assemble: the queer youth autonomy movement. QYA believes that queer and trans youth should be at the forefront of the movement for LGBTQ+ youth liberation. Esmée says, "We're not only battling homophobia and transphobia. We're battling adultism and the fact that most adults think that we're too young to know what's best for us. We want to reverse that narrative that has been created against us. We must have the autonomy to control our own destinies, because ultimately, only we know what is best for ourselves."

Photo courtesy of Michelle Cusolito

ALIA CUSOLITO

"People often underestimate young people, but we're all gathered here to fight for the rights of all youth. . . . We walk out to honor our history. We walk out because we believe that all youth deserve safety and a fulfilling life. We walk out because all youth deserve to thrive in a safe environment. We walk out to uplift the voices of those under direct attack. We walk out to commemorate the members of the GSA council family and other queer and trans youth who can no longer be with us. We walk out to fight back."

—Alia Cusolito, speaking outside the Massachusetts State House, March 31, 2022

PROTESTS & MARCHES

Faith Cardillo (they/them) remembers the start of Valentine's Day in eighth grade being like any other Valentine's Day from childhood, until they received a text from their parents that said another school shooting had happened. The tragedy at Marjory Stoneman Douglas High School enraged and inspired Faith to take action on preventing gun violence. They asked their parents, "What can we do?" Seeing David Hogg, a March for Our Lives founder, on television reminded Faith that they could be vocal and get involved too. Faith attended their first protest in Newark, New Jersey, in March 2018 and by 2021 had begun organizing with their local March for Our Lives chapter in New Jersey.

Faith says, "At thirteen, it was very easy for people to dismiss what I had to say and [they] would always tell me that I was too young to know what I was talking about. Luckily, my family was super encouraging and supportive and drove me to every protest and has helped me overcome all of those adversities."

Many protests and organizing meetings later, Faith connected with Queer Youth Assemble in late 2022. "My approach to activism has shifted to focusing more on youth voices. It is much harder to ignore an issue if the students are the ones who are bringing it to the attention of the adults," which is exactly the approach they took when becoming a lead organizer for the March for Queer and Trans Youth Autonomy in 2023. Less than a year later, Faith founded Bulletproof Pride, an organization working to end gun violence and which highlights the voices of LGBTQIA+ individuals directly impacted by gun violence.

FAITH CARDILLO

"Young people are going to play the biggest role in these movements for queer and trans autonomy and liberation. As much as politicians don't want to admit it, the youth are not going away, and we are getting old enough to vote. If you ignore our voices when we call for action and for justice, we will make sure you can't ignore our ballots in November. The more we vote on local levels, the more the boards of education will represent youth, including the LGBTQIA+ community. The more we sit back and watch, more hateful policies will be put in place. Our power stems from our votes and it is going to grow even more crucial once our youth turn eighteen."

—Faith Cardillo

X GONZÁLEZ AND MARCH FOR OUR LIVES

"We are going to be the kids you read about in textbooks."
—X González (they/them)

As a high school student at Marjory Stoneman Douglas High School in Parkland, Florida, X González (they/them) was outspoken in class and served as president

X GONZÁLEZ

of the Queer Student Alliance. Their shaved head didn't come with immediate approval from their parents—instead, they convinced them with a PowerPoint presentation. X's persuasive and passionate personality defines their style of leadership. In X's senior year, eighty thousand people protested in the streets of Washington, DC. Who led them there? Young people.

X's school had been impacted by the growing epidemic of gun violence in our country. Seventeen of X's peers and teachers were killed on February 14, 2018. During the march that followed, the nation watched as X held six minutes and twenty seconds of excruciating silence representing how long the violence lasted in their school that day. X and their friends created a major movement with #NeverAgain and March for Our Lives.

The twenty-eight founders of March for Our Lives, alongside partnering organizations, successfully orchestrated the largest single-day protest against gun violence in history, and the largest youth protest since anti-war demonstrations decades ago during the Vietnam War. Soon chapters of March for Our Lives emerged across the country. Inspired by the Freedom Riders of the 1960s, March for Our Lives set out on the March for Our Lives: Road to Change Tour in 2018 to actively register more voters, especially young people. The tour visited more than eighty communities in twenty-four states that summer, and registered over fifty thousand new voters. In October 2018, the founders of March for Our Lives released the book *Glimmer of Hope: How Tragedy Sparked a Movement* to share their story and raise funds for the movement. March for Our Lives continues to organize young people through chapters across the country.

QUEER YOUTH ASSEMBLE: "IT'S TIME WE CREATE ONE OF THE LARGEST QUEER YOUTH MARCHES IN HISTORY!"

On December 30, 2022, Queer Youth Assemble announced in an Instagram post: "We're starting a protest!" They detailed their plans for the March for Queer and Trans Youth Autonomy in 2023 in all fifty states and DC, uniting as one. "It's time we create one of the largest queer youth marches in history! Uniting every queer and trans young person under the common goals of safety, autonomy, and joy."

After choosing a date and spreading the word that marches would happen, Queer Youth Assemble hosted listening sessions and sent out a survey to youth all across the country to name their demands. Their mission was loud and clear, and led to three months of organizing across the country with students, organizations, and local community organizers. By the evening of March 30, 2023, all fifty states were confirmed. Following the visibility of the march on national news, over 5,300 people and organizations had signed on to the demands.

In Washington, DC, hundreds of people marched from Columbus Park Circle to the US Capitol on March 31, 2023, with lead organizers holding the banner at the front and chanting: "We're here! We're queer! We won't disappear!" "Black Trans Lives Matter!" "This is what democracy looks like." At the conclusion of the march, sixteen speakers from across the country took to the stage, shouting, singing, chanting, and holding silence, to voice their demands for a future that celebrates all queer and trans young people. In addition to the lead organizers, speakers included Shaplaie Brooks, Samira Burnside,

Ryan Cassata, Tori Cooper, Shea Diamond, Cyn Macias-Gómez, Nik Harris, Jazz Jennings, Sameer Jha, Jamie John, Sawyer Keegan, Elliott Lloyd, Kelley Robinson, and Daniel Trujillo.

Jeremiah Sutherland-Roberts, the photographer for the DC march and a consultant for QYA, says, "The march was exuding queer joy and queer excellence. I was surrounded by so many powerful young queer people, it was exhilarating and motivation for me to work for a better future for LGBTQ+ people. Being in DC was a moment I will never forget."

TRANS PROM

Protest includes celebrating joy too! Libby Gonzales, Daniel Trujillo, Grayson McFerrin, and Hobbes Chukumba were the key planners behind the first-ever transgender youth prom at the US Capitol in Washington, DC, which took place on May 22, 2023. This event aimed to create a space for trans joy and resilience amid ongoing political challenges to trans rights. The prom featured a drag performance by MC Stormie Daie, live music, and a mix of pop and rock anthems by artists. Guests entered through a "Tunnel of Love" inspired by the transgender flag, leading to '70s-inspired decor nodding to the Stonewall uprising. The youth organizers created this event to highlight the pride, joy, and resilience within the trans community, offering a night of celebration and solidarity for trans youth from across the country. Their statement declared, "We gather in celebration of who we are, what we bring to the world, and the freedom, imagination and magic that we represent."

QUEER YOUTH ASSEMBLE DEMANDS

GENERAL

- Codify Title IX to include sexuality, gender identity, and gender expression.
- Support, strengthen, and create a Safe Schools Program for LGBTQ+ Students nationally and statewide in Departments of Education. Require all states to form a state-wide Commission on LGBTQ+ youth that will assist with policy, professional development, and queer & trans youth empowerment.
- Actively include communities being discussed when having conversations about them. This includes young people. We know what we need to feel safe and supported. No conversations or decisions about us without us.
- We call for an end to violence and hatred directed toward all people. We ask for empathy and clear actions to support our queer, trans, BIPOC, and disabled communities who survive every day *despite* the world we live in.

SCHOOLS

- We call for the end to outing and ask for teachers, parents, and peers to maintain confidentiality in regards to others' gender, sexuality, and other aspects of our identities.
- We call for school faculty and staff to undergo mandated LGBTQ+ specific diversity, equity, and inclusion training.
- Schools should create and follow a clear plan for trans students to use chosen names in place of legal names (unless specifically instructed otherwise by the student).
- Designate funding for at least one clearly designated and functioning gender-neutral bathroom at all times, and transition to single-stall and multi-stall gender-neutral bathrooms.
- Teach LGBTQ+, BIPOC, and disabled history as part of existing history classes and Make LGBTQ+ History, BIPOC, and African American History electives accessible for students who want to learn about these communities.

- Require the teaching of LGBTQ+ inclusive sex ed as a part of sex ed courses/curriculums. Sex ed should be comprehensive, culturally competent, developmentally appropriate, trauma- and consent-informed, medically accurate, and inclusive of intersex and disabled experiences.
- Remove dress codes that are racist, sexist, homophobic, transphobic, ableist, nativist, xenophobic, mentalist/sanist, or classist.
- Collect, analyze, and publicize Youth Risk Behavior Survey data from the CDC regarding LGBTQ+ students, including gender identity and expression.

PHYSICAL AND MENTAL HEALTH

LEGAL CHANGES

- Ban all forms of conversion therapy on people of all ages nationwide.
- Require any youth-serving medical or mental health specialist to complete nationally certified training on queer & trans youth.

TRANSITIONING

- Require all practitioners be familiar with and follow the World Professional Association for Transgender Health standards for trans healthcare.
- Fund further trans health research.
- We call for an end to all state-sponsored misinformation on transitioning and gender-affirming healthcare.
- Require all states, all territories, and Washington, DC to have a resource page on the state website to support and advocate for the safety of queer and trans youth.

SPORTS

- Allow transgender athletes to participate on the sports team that corresponds with their identity, and provide middle and high schools with state funding for co-ed sports teams.
- Ban genital checks and other invasive, unnecessary medical practices for all athletes.

POLICY

- Pass the Equality Act HR5
- Require states to form an LGBTQ+ legislative group to advise lawmakers on legislation that impacts the LGBTQ+ community
- Create a federal law protecting the right to healthcare and bodily autonomy for trans youth and adults.
- Ratify the Equality Amendment, an updated comprehensive and inclusive version of the proposed federal Equal Rights Amendment, which would protect the equal rights of all peoples and prohibit any and all forms of discrimination based on race, ethnicity, sexual orientation, gender identity, nationality, disability, religion, spirituality, etc.
- Ratify Equality Amendments into state constitutions or update current state Equal Rights Amendments to make them fully comprehensive and inclusive.
- Repeal any and all existing state constitutional amendments banning same-sex unions and replace them with marriage equality amendments.
- Repeal any and all existing state anti-sodomy laws that are still on the legal books.

WORKPLACES

- Create a federal law protecting queer & trans people's rights and safety in the workplace.

"In the face of our current national climate, it's easy to feel powerless as a young person. But being at the March, side by side with so many incredible organizers, and seeing hundreds of people coming out in support was a tangible reminder of just how powerful our voices can be."
    —Alex Nugent, QYA Head of Volunteer Support

ESMÉE SILVERMAN

"Together we will create a world where all queer and trans youth are safe! Where the suicide rate is down to zero. Where violence and discrimination are things of the past. We will create a world where all queer and trans youth are able to make the decisions that impact them! Where youth are not forced to be activists, but can pursue their dreams as artists, chefs, filmmakers, and farmers. We will create a world where all queer and trans youth are full of joy. Where radiating smiles of youth seeing their authentic self in the mirror for the first time is a common occurrence. We will create a world where adults do not assume what queer and trans youth are, but rather ask queer and trans youth who they are. We will create a world where access to hormones is easier than access to guns."

—Esmée Silverman, speaking at the DC March for Queer and Trans Youth Autonomy

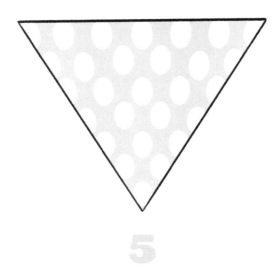

5

ACTIONS FOR YOUTH

What brings you joy and hope? Who are your supportive people, and how do you stay connected with them? What are some ways you practice self care and community care?

You have likely seen something about yourself reflected in the stories of the activists here, not only because of their advocacy but in the ways they prioritize joy. Maybe you find joy in connecting with your favorite people, or you love playing video games, or your cat calms you down every day after school.

Whether you've organized actions in your community or are still learning how you want to express yourself, the feelings that many of these youth activists highlighted around envisioning a better future likely resonated with you: taking care of ourselves and each other, and reflecting on who we are and what that means when we interact with other people.

I want to remind you that you are brilliant as you are. Your worth is not determined by what you produce, or by how other people perceive you. You get to decide who you are, what brings

FOLLOW YOUR CURIOSITY, AND MEANINGFUL CONNECTIONS AND OPPORTUNITIES WILL EMERGE.

you joy, and how you want to express yourself. Your voice is valuable and needed. At the same time, you deserve a full childhood of exploration, fun, and curiosity. You are not responsible for the mistakes of adults, or the failures you may be inheriting. As you do what you can to create a better future for yourself and your friends, please know that there are so many people behind you and alongside you. Even in moments when your town feels isolating, or you don't know how to get through the day, there is someone who loves you, but most important, you can practice love for yourself. We have so much to fight and to dismantle and to unravel, and one way we can do that is through celebrating joy, connection, and community.

As you move forward in your own journey as a human, activist, artist, educator, friend, sibling, and so much more, I want to leave you with some more extended quotes and stories from the passionate people who were interviewed for this book. You'll also find plenty of resources, including

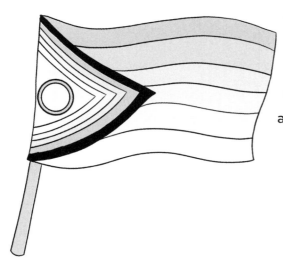

national organizations that I encourage you to explore, reach out to, and learn the history of. Remember, follow your curiosity, and meaningful connections and opportunities will emerge.

ON ENVISIONING THE FUTURE . . .

JOSHUA ALLEN

"So in my own experience, I've always found that young people are maybe the most invested in change-making, because we're the ones that are gonna be living in the world we're fighting so hard to change. I also think that there's a level of joy and excitement in redefining the ways that the world around us is shaped, because frankly, young people, we didn't ask to be here, no one signed up. So I think that there's a level of joy and excitement and freedom that comes in being able to redefine the rules, particularly around sexuality and gender, because they were given to us so rigidly and we can mold them and shape them however we want to. And so I think that young people, of course historically, have had a huge role to play and I think that this generation is no different than anyone that came before us: fighting just to make things a little bit easier, the world a little bit more free, open, and beautiful for all of us to enjoy."

—Joshua Allen

ZANDER MORICZ

"As legislation targets queer and trans youth more than ever before, it is essential that queer and trans youth are given the opportunity to direct the response. The problem is that while members of older generations are often willing to elevate the youth voice, they are rarely willing to act on what they hear. Most high-level organizations that lead the queer community are run by adults. Due to the inherent lack of experience that accompanies young age, young people are rarely allowed to be meaningful stakeholders in political movements. Therefore, deprived of the resources and connections needed to create true and lasting change,

Gen Z has found a last resort in social media. But most digital activism informs without informing on how to act. Social media connects people from many different places to many different issues, but does not provide the structure or systems to impactfully address each one. The resulting product is a culture where activists give bursts of attention to problems as they arise in the media, and the American media is both fickle and overflowing with crises to share. So because young digital activists are constantly trying to stay relevant and engaged, their organizing is reminiscent of simply following trends. This fails to bring about lasting progress—a fact many are beginning to recognize. As we look to the future of activism, and the role that the incoming generation will play in shaping it, the question must be: How can social media expand the impact of grassroots organizing?" —Zander Moricz

SOMAH HAALAND

"I feel like it's so important for us all to keep imagining this collective future together. Liberation will only happen if we bring everyone with us, even those people that think of themselves as separate from us." —Somah Haaland

ESMÉE SILVERMAN

"We believe that queer youth deserve the right to make their own choices. There are choices that queer youth should be guaranteed, like the right to receive affirming medical care, the ability to join the sports team they feel most comfortable on, the freedom to say who they are in school, the basic human right to exist. We want our queer youth to have the power to do whatever their hearts desire, and we believe that through resources, professional guidance, connecting with queer youth, support groups, and time to process their thoughts, they're able to make decisions safely and effectively. That's one of our main focuses here, is that we want to offer action steps for autonomizing queer youth." —Esmée Silverman

SAMEER JHA

"Youth can also be less willing to work within a problematic system because they've spent less time in that system, and so they're willing to think of more radical ideas and believe that those things can happen. So it's that optimism that you can completely change the world. And, you know, that's something I noticed with myself as well, the more time I spend in the world, and having to just interact with the world the way it is, the more I get used to some things that I think my younger counterparts are completely shocked and appalled by." —Sameer Jha

ON PRIVILEGE AND WHOSE STORIES ARE TOLD . . .

MEG LEE

"I've learned so much throughout my journey on social media and stepping into such an activist space. The biggest thing I've learned and continue to apply to the work I do is knowing when I deserve to take up space and when I need to take a step back and amplify and uplift someone else or another community altogether. It is crucial and so important that I continue to put thought, time, energy, and positive intent into everything I post on social media to make sure that I am acknowledging my privilege, intent, and always centering my work around amplifying and uplifting the voices and lives of folks who are often left in the shadows. My activism work often includes my own Asian American trans nonbinary experiences, but also must *always* include Black trans folks and specifically Black trans women who are targeted the most." —Meg Lee

SOMAH HAALAND

"The challenge is just being continuously mindful that the work is never over. But also I'm not going to be perfect, so sometimes I might say things that I'm going to have to correct later. But I feel like part of this work is normalizing changing your mind when you learn new information, and admitting when you've made a mistake." —Somah Haaland

SARA K. DUNN

"I try to uplift others and also recognize my privilege as a white woman. White women have dominated spaces for a long time, particularly in the art world. I want to make sure that other people get the chance and are recognized for their work. I used to give back in a more broad sense and support bigger organizations, but then I realized I would rather support local people's GoFundMes, or Venmo someone who is in need on their stories, or something where it's just much more one or two people removed instead of a big conglomerate nonprofit that just doesn't really get to the communities that really matter. So I think that was another important thing I've learned along the way. Also supporting other artists that I care about. I try to buy prints, or other things from people when I can support them and the beautiful things that they create." —Sara K. Dunn

REEVES GIFT

"Something I've realized is super important to me is to make sure people who aren't living in huge coastal cities aren't forgotten. People don't always understand the bubble they're in. I want to make stories about queer people in those places so they're not forgotten. It's okay to like where you come from. There's a lot of pride in being out and open in areas where it's a problem. It's the worst thing to be an LGBTQ person dealing with so-called progressive people who look at me and assume things about where I'm from—it's definitely not the worst thing to be from where I'm from (Maryland and Trinidad). I want to create content for people to understand that it's not easy *and* there's so much pride. It requires so much strength that many people don't understand." —Reeves Gift

REBEKAH BRUESEHOFF

"I definitely try to be really careful and aware of how much space I'm taking up as a white person who identifies within the gender binary. And I think it's really important to just recognize how much privilege I have and to be able to step back for other people who have voices that aren't heard as much. I'm constantly learning from what other activists like me are doing and how they are doing the work they do and how they're passionate about it, and I don't think that's specifically for LGBTQ+ activists, it's for activists around immigration rights, disabilities, neurodiversity, and so forth." —Rebekah Bruesehoff

ON THE IMPORTANCE OF FINDING YOUR COMMUNITY AND CHOSEN FAMILY . . .

MARI WROBI

"Currently in my life, everyone that I know and I'm friends with knows that I'm intersex, knows that I'm queer, knows that I'm nonbinary, knows I use they/them pronouns. There's no one in my life that doesn't know those things and I feel like that is the most healing experience of all: not having to hide anymore and not having to be silent anymore." —Mari Wrobi

ZANDER MORICZ

"I think it is important to recognize that most coming-out stories aren't perfect. My family loves me, and always has, yet we had to work and grow to reach a place where I could happily be myself. Only hearing absolutely perfect or absolutely terrible coming-out stories delayed my process significantly, because I knew it wouldn't be the former and I didn't want to risk the latter. When I did come out, I recognized the truth: quite like sexuality, coming out exists on a spectrum. Your timing and reactions will be different than everyone else's—focus on your peace and safety above all else." —Zander Moricz

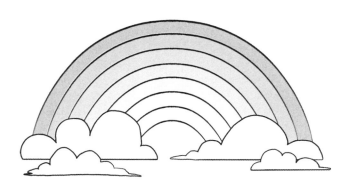

SHANNON LI

"If you're in a situation where it's very challenging, seek out people that you consider safe and also will provide you safe space. I think oftentimes we get so bogged down and overwhelmed by people who don't agree with us, who may make discriminatory comments about our identities. There are also those individuals out there that you may have access to that are very supportive, and can really be a lifeline for you. Even just having one person in your life that is able to support you goes a long way. I would also say to take charge of our own story. Be able to write your own story out the way you want it to be and take charge of that." —Shannon Li

ON TRUSTING OURSELVES AND OUR WISDOM . . .

SHERENTÉ MISHITASHIN HARRIS

"Violence is something that cannot really be destroyed. It can only be transformed. Violence travels from one individual to another, and it can transform through different avenues, but I think the same thing exists for empowerment. When you empower people, that goes far beyond just that individual action, but has ripple effects where it will then change the course of so many other people's lives beyond what you know. This is an ancient sacred wisdom that our [Narragansett] people have always held when we think about the seven generations. The idea of the seven generations being that [in] everything that we do, we should not just think about how it will affect the generation that comes after us, or two or three generations, but you think about how that will affect the next seven generations to come. When we look behind us, to look not only to the teachings of our parents or our grandparents, but to carry with us the wisdom of the seven generations." —Sherenté Mishitashin Harris

RYAN CASSATA

"I want you to know that you know who you are. No adults can take that away from you. Every situation you're in right now, that's really hard—whether it's people bullying you, or your parents—you aren't stuck in that situation forever, and you do get to get older and have the freedom to choose your path more. You need to hold on. I get being a trans youth, and I get having laws that are attacking you, and I feel that so heavily in my heart. I see you and hear you. I feel you, you're all in my heart and I am here in this fight. A lot of us are willing to sacrifice and step up to the plate to protect trans youth, and we're working on that every single day. So really, just hold on and keep being yourself, keep being true."
—Ryan Cassata

SOMAH HAALAND

"I recently participated in a panel discussion with the Williams Institute at UCLA, and there was a moment where I was really doubting myself. I was like, I don't know as much as these people, but the facilitator of the panel took time to talk to me, and I realized that my experience is valuable. It helped me ground myself and feel like I have things to bring to these spaces, even if I don't know something. That's also another tool of oppression: to make us feel like we're not smart enough when we really are so I was proud of myself for getting through and following through with that, and I'm hoping to do more things like that in the future."
—Somah Haaland

JESS GUILBEAUX

"For queer youth, just don't get in your own way. I feel like it's really easy to subscribe to what society tells us we can be, and what society tells us that we can do and achieve. You know, if I could go back ten years and tell her everything that I've been able to do, I probably wouldn't have even listened. It's definitely hindsight. Just try not to get in your own head, and in your own way, because you are capable of more than you even thought possible, and I mean that the least cliché way because it's actually true." —Jess Guilbeaux

ESMÉE SILVERMAN

"If somebody ever tells you that you're too young to do something, don't listen to them. I'm twenty years old and I run a nonprofit with 180 people in twenty-six different states. Don't let other people's expectations of you determine what you do in your life. It is your life. They are your ambitions: you go out there, and show the world what you can do, what you are capable of. If you're a queer youth organizer or if you want to get into organizing, then go and organize something. If you want to walk out because your school is being homophobic, then walk out. Don't let ageism dictate what you are capable of, because you are truly capable of anything you put your mind to."

—Esmée Silverman

ON TAKING CARE OF OURSELVES AND PREVENTING BURNOUT . . .

MARI WROBI

"I also learned to take a second to myself to just be like, okay, maybe I don't have the spoons or the energy to create like twenty TikToks in a day. I still felt so bad when I had to say no to people, and that was sort of my own lesson and realizing that I can focus on myself a little bit more. I will look at my TikToks and answer comments and questions, and at a certain point, I'll be like, all right, I'm done for the night. Learning those things really was kind of a turning point for me in my activism, where I learned there's a strategy to being an activist, and I don't have to have the candle burning at both ends in order for it to be meaningful and impactful work." —Mari Wrobi

JP GRANT

"I have learned to become selfish and work on myself in order to help others. And so I think that being selfish has actually allowed me to actually strive more and actually be able to get more and pour more into my communities, whereas I was pouring into things or partnerships that didn't really uplift my work or uplift my needs as well. So being able to be selective in where you put your time and energy. That's definitely been hard, but something that I've been able to do and put my foot down." —JP Grant

FAITH CARDILLO

"My work in activism can get really heavy and depressing since my expertise is in gun violence prevention, human rights, and voting rights. For self care, I've learned that writing poetry and reading have been my favorite creative outlet. Reading books with queer representation and publishing poems with aro-ace representation has given me another replenishing sense of purpose outside of activism." —Faith Cardillo

MARI WROBI

"Before, I said yes to everything. Any time I was approached, like any time somebody wanted to do an interview, or wanted to do a story, or wanted me to come talk to their class, I remember saying yes to every single thing. And what I didn't realize, that later became a topic of discussion just within the intersex community in general, was that a lot of the people that I was saying yes to were people who were actually exploiting me and my story. And that wasn't something that I had on my radar initially, but through talking with my fellow activists and especially fellow young activists, I remember that I started to see intersex youth activists put their foot down and say, 'Actually, no, we're not going to just exploit ourselves and our stories.' And I also had to learn a few lessons in the burnout that comes with advocacy work, because by saying yes to everything, I was also kind of just running myself into the ground. That's actually a pretty common issue within the intersex community is like the publicness of our stories versus like the things that we want and deserve to keep private." —Mari Wrobi

ON EMBRACING JOY RIGHT NOW . . .

JOSHUA ALLEN

"Maybe one of the biggest realizations that I've been having over the last couple of years is that so much of my time as a community organizer I thought that I kind of need to fight and struggle to make something, like it's the destination that I'm trying to get to. I think what I realize now, maybe as I'm getting smarter or more mature, I realize that there's no destination I'm going to, this is all a journey, and that I'm living it every single day. And so the ability to find joy, to find freedom, to find excitement, happiness, community, togetherness, those are all things that I'm going to experience the rest of my life. It's not like a hill that I'm trying to get over, it's something that exists right now. And so I think that having that shift in mindset, and it's still shifting, has been extremely important, because I think it opens up a level of possibility, and love and joy, that I think I deserve and I think that all of us deserve. And so as an activist it's something that I've been working to change every day, to stop thinking, 'Oh I'm fighting for this, I'm fighting for that'; I'm fighting for right now, the things that I want in the world, they're already mine, and I have to just kind of walk into them."
—Joshua Allen

MALLERY JENNA ROBINSON

"One of my favorite sayings is, 'Be better, not bitter.' I've had things said about me for my race, to my gender, to my HIV status, and if I let those things deter me, I don't think I would be able to be here with you. So that is always just my message of hope to all of our queer and trans youth. That is just to continue to persevere. Keep that resilience, and maintain that tenacity, you know? And just remember, be better, not bitter because you know you're gonna come out on the other side." —Mallery Jenna Robinson

NATIONAL ORGANIZATIONS

These are national organizations that are youth-led or youth-centered. Explore their websites to learn more about the work they're doing to uplift LGBTQ+ youth.

Asexual Outreach (asexualoutreach.org) is a nonprofit organization that works in Canada and the United States to foster positive ace community, education, and acceptance. Asexual Outreach also started Aces & Aros in 2016 to prioritize equitable inclusion of aromantic content.

BlackLine (1-800-604-5841) provides peer support and counseling to those most impacted by systematic oppression, particularly LGBTQ+ Black femme folks.

CenterLink (lgbtcenters.org) is an international nonprofit organization and network of LGBTQ centers and organizations serving their local and regional communities.

COLAGE (colage.org) is a national movement of children, youth, and adults with one or more LGBTQ parents.

DAY Prism (dearasianyouth.org/prism) is an Asian youth-led group dedicated to advocating for LGBTQ+ youth.

Deaf Queer Resource Center (deafqueer.org) is a Deaf QTPOC LGBTQ-led nonprofit organization based in California. They host Deaf LGBTQ Awareness Week every year in April.

Future Perfect Project (thefutureperfectproject.com) creates safe spaces for LGBTQ+ youth and allies to express themselves through the arts, social connections, and amplifying their voices.

GSA Network (gsanetwork.org) is a next-generation LGBTQ racial and gender justice organization that empowers and trains queer, trans, and allied youth leaders through a network of GSAs nationwide.

interACT Youth (interactadvocates.org) is the world's largest intersex advocacy group for youth ages thirteen to twenty-nine.

It Gets Better Project (itgetsbetter.org) is a nonprofit organization with a mission to uplift, empower, and connect LGBTQ youth around the globe.

Learning for Justice (learningforjustice.org) works to be a catalyst for racial justice in the South and beyond. Their website provides free educational materials and curricula focused on social justice topics.

March for Our Lives (marchforourlives.com) is a youth-led movement promoting civic engagement, education, and direct action by youth to eliminate the epidemic of gun violence.

Muslim Youth Leadership Council (advocatesforyouth.org/about/our -programs/muslim-youth-leadership-council-mylc) is a group of Muslim-identifying people ages seventeen to twenty-four from across the country, working locally and nationally to promote LGBTQ rights, immigrant rights, and sexual and reproductive health and rights for Muslims.

Native Youth Sexual Health Network (nativeyouthsexualhealth.com) is a grassroots network of Indigenous youth and intergenerational relatives.

Point Foundation (pointfoundation.org) is the nation's largest scholarship-granting organization for LGBTQ+ students.

Prism Foundation (theprismfoundation.org) provides scholarships to empower Asian and Pacific Islander LGBTQ+ students and communities.

Q Chat Space (qchatspace.org) is a digital LGBTQ+ center where you can join professionally facilitated discussion groups for teens.

Queer Youth Assemble (queeryouthassemble.org) works to bring joy and autonomy to all queer youth under twenty-five in the United States and territories.

SMYAL (smyal.org) creates opportunities for LGBTQ youth to build self-confidence, develop critical life skills, access transitional housing, and engage their community through service and advocacy.

Trans Lifeline (translifeline.org) is a trans-led organization that offers a hotline, legal support, and funds directly to trans people.

Trans Women of Color Collective (twocc.org) is working to uplift the narratives, lived experiences, and leadership of trans and gender nonconforming people of color.

The Trevor Project (thetrevorproject.org) is the world's largest suicide prevention and crisis intervention organization for LGBTQ+ young people.

True Colors United (truecolorsunited.org) implements innovative solutions to LGBTQ youth homelessness.

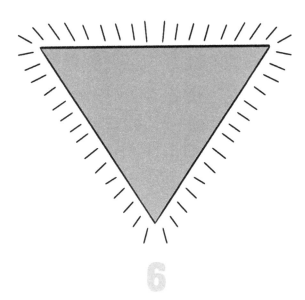

6

ACTIONS FOR EDUCATORS

Can you think of an educator who was influential in your life? How did you know you could trust them? What showed you that they were consistent, and would show up for you fully and authentically? What were the qualities of that educator that made you feel welcomed, included, and confident in your own learning?

Often our role as educators is to signal to young people that we can offer nonjudgmental safety and care. Without that feeling of safety, meaningful learning is hard to achieve. If you're reading this book, or have LGBTQ+ books in your classroom or library, you're already signaling to LGBTQ+ young people that you are making an effort to be there for them. If you're a GSA advisor or lead an LGBTQIA+ affinity space in your school, thank you for creating this needed resource and opportunity for connection.

Now think back to the first time that you learned about LGBTQ+ people and their contributions to our society in an educational setting. Not from your friends or family, but in an educational setting like a classroom. What was it that you learned? Most often, when I ask groups of educators this question, the answer is a resounding "never and nothing," or it wasn't until much later in their education, or in interacting with a student now, as an educator. Because we grew up either hearing negative messages about LGBTQ+ people or experiencing silence and erasure, we likely hold implicit biases now as adults. One place for all of us to start is to examine our own biases and privileges, and how they might subtly show up in our classrooms. We can also hold that while these issues are urgent, we can be patient and kind with ourselves when we make mistakes. These are moments to model growth, learning, and humility.

Having a rainbow sticker or books featuring LGBTQ+ characters in your school is one way to signal safety. But a signal always needs to be paired with action. I've heard from students that it can feel performative when a rainbow sticker is on a teacher's door, yet homophobic or transphobic slurs are ignored, and LGBTQ+ people are never included in the curriculum. Students are looking for visible signs that they belong—and that educators will have their backs when harm is done, and will prevent harm in the first place. As LGBTQ+ people navigate hearing microaggressions or harmful comments, we can interrupt that, provide comfort and support, and also counter that with microaffirmations—those small comments or gestures that let people know they are seen and valued by us. This could be a compliment on the shoes they're wearing that they clearly love,

TRANSFORMING YOUR SCHOOL BEGINS WITH UNDERSTANDING THE BARRIERS AND OPPORTUNITIES THAT EXIST RIGHT NOW—AND WHAT NEEDS TO BE DONE TO BETTER PROTECT YOUNG PEOPLE.

acknowledgment of how awesome their name is, or an appreciation for how they take care of themselves and prioritize their mental health.

MARI WROBI

"I remember the first time that somebody bought me an ornament that had my chosen name on it. It was this tiny thing that probably cost like two dollars, and it got me through probably the entire holiday season because I was like, 'Oh my god, somebody actually sees me for the person that I am, the person that I see myself as.'"
—Mari Wrobi

LGBTQ+ students are often navigating schools and systems that were never built for them. They need the support of adults like you to transform those systems and ensure that all young people are protected. We can see the brilliance in all our students and serve them not as saviors, but as partners in their growth, joy, and self-discovery. When attacks on LGBTQ+ youth are happening all over the country through legislation, hate crimes, and discrimination, it is our role to speak up, provide support, and debunk misinformation. Young people notice when we are silent on the issues most seriously impacting their lives and futures. Of course, this comes with inherent risks in states with discriminatory legislation, and educators are in need of just as much support as they navigate these difficult political challenges.

Transforming your school begins with understanding the barriers and opportunities that exist right now—and what needs to be done to better protect young people. Gender Inclusive

DAYS AND MONTHS OF RECOGNITION

While the contributions of LGBTQ+ people should be celebrated all year and included in all curricula, these are some special days and months of recognition that you can highlight as themes for units or lesson plans.

SEPTEMBER 15–OCTOBER 15: National Hispanic Heritage Month

OCTOBER: LGBTQ History Month

OCTOBER 11: National Coming Out Day

OCTOBER 26: Intersex Awareness Day

NOVEMBER: Native American Heritage Month

NOVEMBER 20: Transgender Day of Remembrance

NOVEMBER (fourth Thursday): National Day of Mourning

DECEMBER 1: World AIDS Day

FEBRUARY: Black History Month

FEBRUARY (first full week): Black Lives Matter at School Week of Action

MARCH: Women's History Month

MARCH 31: Transgender Day of Visibility

APRIL: Deaf History Month

APRIL: Day of Silence (exact date TBD every year by GLSEN)

APRIL: National Deaf LGBTQ Awareness Week (exact date TBD every year by Deaf Queer Resource Center)

MAY: Asian American, Native Hawaiian, and Pacific Islanders Heritage Month

MAY (first full week): Teacher Appreciation Week

MAY 17: International Day Against Homophobia, Transphobia, and Biphobia

JUNE: Caribbean American Heritage Month

JUNE: LGBTQI+ Pride Month

JUNE 18: Autistic Pride Day

JULY: Disability Pride Month

Schools and the Movement Advancement Project both have maps of school policies in the United States that you can explore to learn more about the policies within your state. With hundreds of anti-LGBTQ bills being introduced each year, it is crucial that we counter those harmful attempts to erase us with better protections, policies, and school cultures to support youth. Find out if your school or district has a GSA, or another inclusion-based student group, and ask them how you can support their work if you're not already involved.

We know that one supportive adult can make the difference in whether an LGBTQ+ young person will survive. Using a student's chosen name and pronouns reduces the risk of suicide and depression. Inclusive curriculum, accessible all-gender bathrooms, visibly out educators, and anti-discrimination policies are also connected to improved school climates, student engagement in school, and overall mental health and well-being for LGBTQ+ youth. People often find these facts surprising, maybe because the antidotes are so simple. The more adults who can push beyond their fear of making a mistake or coming up against opposition, and instead move toward learning and embracing the strengths of LGBTQ+ youth, the better off our young people and schools will be.

Having a loving and supportive relationship with a parent or caregiver is also incredibly important. Educators can help build bridges between youth and families. Resources like PFLAG and the Family Acceptance Project are focused on building these relationships. Sometimes it can benefit a parent to meet another parent or family member of a trans child with shared cultural experiences, for example, to talk through their questions.

FAITH CARDILLO

"I grew up in a very loving and accepting family. I was able to have conversations about my sexuality and all the confusion that came with it at a very young age. I was able to ask my siblings and my parents questions like: 'Why do I like girls but not guys?' or 'Is it okay to have a crush on a girl?' Reflecting on everything, I think a huge aspect of why I am able to do the advocacy work I do is because my brain isn't constantly on survival mode. I am able to advocate for others who are surviving, since I'm not in that mindset and [am] in a supportive environment around me."
—Faith Cardillo

You likely have so many allies in your community, even if the opposition feels overwhelming. As I mentioned in the introduction, we're all lifelong learners, and as educators, we can model a growth mindset for students and our colleagues. Let's follow the lead of young people rather than be fearful. There are some great resources here to help support work in your classroom and in your school, including days of recognition/celebration, organizations, and books. I hope these will lead you to affirming and celebratory stories, policies, and people who will ultimately allow your school community to be safer for all youth.

NATIONAL ORGANIZATIONS AND RESOURCES

These are national organizations that are advocating for LGBTQ+ people. Explore their websites to learn more about the work they're doing in legal advocacy, mental health support, family engagement, inclusive curriculum, and much more.

500 Queer Scientists (500queerscientists.com) is a visibility campaign representing LGBTQ+ people and their allies working in STEM.

ACLU (aclu.org) advocates for equal rights, personal autonomy, and freedom of expression for LGBTQ people.

ACT UP (actupny.com) is a direct action organization formed in the 1980s to create an end to the AIDS crisis.

Advocates for Trans Equality (transequality.org) advocates to change policies and society to increase understanding and acceptance of transgender people.

Athlete Ally (athleteally.org) is working to end homophobia and transphobia in sports through education, advocacy, and policy-making.

Black Emotional and Mental Health Collective (beam.community) is a national organization that enhances access to mental healthcare for Black and marginalized communities through education, training, advocacy, and arts.

Familia TQLM (familiatqlm.org) is working to achieve the collective liberation of trans, queer, and gender-nonconforming Latinxs through local and national efforts to build community, organize, advocate, and educate.

The Family Acceptance Project (familyproject.sfsu.edu) creates research, intervention, education, and policy initiatives focused on LGBTQ children and youth in the context of their families, cultures, and faith communities.

Gender Inclusive Biology (genderinclusivebiology.com) creates resources for a more inclusive biology curriculum.

Gender Spectrum (genderspectrum.org) provides education, training, and support to help people better understand gender. They are the authors of the Gender Support Plan tool, which provides schools with helpful questions and guidance for supporting transgender students.

GLAD (glad.org) works in New England and nationally on behalf of LGBTQ people, and is a leader in legal justice.

GLSEN (glsen.org) is a national network of educators, students, local GLSEN chapters, and education advocates working for safe, supportive, and LGBTQ-inclusive K–12 education.

History UnErased (unerased.org) is an education nonprofit bringing LGBTQ US history into the mainstream curriculum in K–12 schools.

Hope in a Box (hopeinabox.org) provides public school educators with LGBTQ-inclusive literature and curricula, as well as training on how to build LGBTQ-inclusive classrooms.

Keshet (keshetonline.org) advocates for full equality of LGBTQ Jews and their families in Jewish life.

Lambda Literary (lambdaliterary.org) nurtures and advocates for LGBTQ writers.

Lanechanger (lanechanger.com) is an online learning experience with over forty video modules and quizzes about gender and transgender topics developed by Schuyler Bailar.

Marsha P. Johnson Institute (marshap.org) protects and defends the human rights of Black transgender people through organizing, advocacy, creating intentional communities, developing transformative leadership, and promoting collective power.

Matthew Shepard Foundation (matthewshepard.org) amplifies the story of Matthew Shepard to inspire individuals, organizations, and communities to embrace the dignity and equality of all people.

Movement Advancement Project (lgbtmap.org) is a nonprofit providing rigorous research, insight, and communications to advance equality and opportunity for all.

National Coalition of Anti-Violence Programs (avp.org/ncavp) works to prevent, respond to, and end all forms of violence against and within LGBTQ communities.

National Queer & Trans Therapists of Color Network (nqttcn.com) is a healing justice organization committed to transforming mental health for queer and trans people of color.

The Network / La Red (tnlr.org) is a survivor-led social justice organization that works to end partner abuse. TNLR has a twenty-four-hour hotline.

Okra Project (theokraproject.com) is a mutual aid collective that supports Black trans people.

One Institute (oneinstitute.org/education) provides educational programs and resources focused on the transformative stories of LGBTQ history.

PFLAG (pflag.org) provides confidential peer support, education, and advocacy to LGBTQ+ people, their parents and families, and their allies.

SIECUS (siecus.org) advocates for people's right to accurate and comprehensive sexuality information, education, and related health services.

SOJOURN (sojourngsd.org), the Southern Jewish Resource Network for Gender and Sexual Diversity, is empowering communities to advance and celebrate gender and sexual diversity across the South.

Somos Familia (somosfamiliabay.com) is a Spanish-language interactive web experience that guides Latinx families through videos, articles, and personal accounts of the LGBTQ+ community.

Sylvia Rivera Law Project (srlp.org) is a collective organization working to raise the political voice of low-income people and people of color who are trans, intersex, and/or gender non-conforming.

Tegan and Sara Foundation (teganandsarafoundation.org) is working to improve the lives of LGBTQ+ women and girls through community grants and programming.

Transgender Law Center (transgenderlawcenter.org) was originally a project of the National Center for Lesbian Rights, and is now the largest trans-led organization in the US impacting laws and policy that affect transgender people.

TransLatin@ Coalition (translatinacoalition.org) was founded in 2009 by a group of transgender and gender-nonconforming and intersex (TGI) immigrant women in Los Angeles. It provides direct services and resources to TGI Latin@ immigrants.

Trans People of Color Coalition (transpocc.org) is a nonprofit organization promoting the interests of trans people of color.

Trans Student Educational Resources (transstudent.org) is a youth-led organization dedicated to transforming the educational environment for trans and gender nonconforming students through advocacy and empowerment.

Welcoming Schools (welcomingschools.org) is a bias-based bullying prevention program providing LGBTQ+ and gender-inclusive professional development, curricula, book lists, and resources specifically designed for educators and youth-serving professionals.

MORE BOOKS

There have been a ton of book recommendations included throughout the earlier chapters of *Generation Queer*. Here are some final additions of fantastic reads for children and young adults, as well as adult nonfiction.

CHILDREN'S AND YOUNG ADULT BOOKS

How We Can Live | Laleña Garcia, illustrated by Caryn Davidson, Lee & Low Books, 2022.

It Feels Good to Be Yourself: A Book about Gender Identity | Theresa Thorn, illustrated by Noah Grigni, Henry Holt and Co., 2019.

Juliet Takes a Breath | Gabby Rivera, Dial Books, 2019.

King and the Dragonflies | Kacen Callender, Scholastic, 2020.

Pet | Akwaeke Emezi, Make Me a World, 2019.

Red at the Bone | Jacqueline Woodson, Riverhead Books, 2019.

This Is Our Rainbow: 16 Stories of Her, Him, Them, and Us | Ed. Katherine Locke and Nicole Melleby, Knopf Books for Young Readers, 2021.

When Aidan Became a Brother | Kyle Lukoff, illustrated by Kaylani Juanita, Lee & Low Books, 2019.

Cover courtesy of Lee & Low Books Inc.

NONFICTION

Black Lives Matter at School: An Uprising for Educational Justice | Ed. Denisha Jones & Jesse Hagopian, Haymarket Books, 2020.

Black on Both Sides: A Racial History of Trans Identity | C. Riley Snorton, University of Minnesota Press, 2017.

Histories of the Transgender Child | Julian Gill-Peterson, University of Minnesota Press, 2018.

The New Queer Conscience | Adam Eli, Penguin Workshop, 2020.

No Sanctuary: Teachers and the School Reform That Brought Gay Rights to the Masses | Stephen Lane, ForeEdge, 2018.

A Quick & Easy Guide to They/Them Pronouns | Archie Bongiovanni and Tristan Jimerson, Limerence Press, 2018.

Reclaiming Two-Spirits: Sexuality, Spiritual Renewal & Sovereignty in Native America | Gregory D. Smithers, Beacon Press, 2022.

Rethinking Sexism, Gender, and Sexuality | Rethinking Schools, 2016.

The Stonewall Reader | Ed. New York Public Library, Penguin Classics, 2019.

Supporting Transgender Autistic Youth and Adults | Finn V. Gratton, Jessica Kingsley, 2019.

This Bridge Called My Back: Writings by Radical Women of Color | Ed. Cherríe Moraga and Gloria E. Anzaldúa, State University of New York, 2021.

ACKNOWLEDGMENTS

This book is a dream in the making for many years—and it's a representation of the enduring support, guidance, and encouragement of so many people.

First and foremost, I am endlessly grateful to all the people who were interviewed for this book. Your stories and voices deserve celebration—and I will forever be honored that you trusted me with this process. Thank you for all the time, energy, stories, humor, and patience you shared. I hope you feel proud reading this book.

My deepest gratitude goes to my incredible agent, Lauren Scovel, whose belief in this project from the very beginning helped shape it into what it is today. Thank you, Lauren, for being such a phenomenal advocate for this book and envisioning it in the world.

I am immensely grateful to my editor, Stacy Whitman, and the entire Tu Books team for their unwavering dedication, insightful feedback, and tireless efforts in bringing this book to life. Your guidance and wisdom, Stacy, allowed me to transform and reimagine this book again and again. Thanks also to the entire Tu Books editorial team, particularly managing editor Melissa Kavonic, copyeditor Chandra Wohleber, and proofreader Stevonnie Ross, for all your detailed feedback.

To Anshika Khullar, your illustrations brought this book to life in ways I could only dream of. Thank you for capturing the energy and passion of these stories so beautifully.

A heartfelt thank you to E.B. Bartels, who provided invaluable guidance and feedback on the early drafts of the book proposal. Your transparency and generosity gave me the confidence I needed.

I am also deeply appreciative of Ella McKenzie and Ari Hartley for their assistance with transcriptions and enthusiasm for the heart of this project.

To my incredible friends and colleagues who read the earliest drafts and offered constant encouragement—Alia, Angela, Annie, Arushi, Asha, Billy, Brimar, Cas, Esmée, Ev, Indra, Jenn, Joha, Julie, Ke, Landon, Lyv, Max, Meghan, MG, Molly, Nana, Puja, Sabrina, Samyuktha, Sawyer, Shae, Sky, Travis—thank you. Your feedback was so meaningful, and your friendship kept me grounded and always grateful to be in community with such amazing people.

To the organizations that shaped my approach to this work and taught me how to organize with compassion and intention—The Network / La Red, the Safe Schools Program for LGBTQ Students, Trans Resistance, and Tutoring Plus.

To my mentors over the years—Albert Liau, Aren Stone, Brian Becker, Deb Fowler, Ellen McLaughlin, Emily Shield, Gilda Bruckman, Gretchen Brion-Meisels, Jeff Perrotti, Kathryn Fenneman, Kimberly Sansoucy, Michael Venturiello, Michelle Cusolito, Nakia Navarro, Timothy McCarthy, Tre'Andre Carmel Valentine—thank you for your guidance, wisdom, and care. Your influence has meant the world to me.

Finally, to my younger self, you did it! You are always pushing yourself gently to become the person you needed.

This book is a testament to the collective efforts of a remarkable community, and I am deeply thankful for each and every one of you.

ABOUT THE AUTHOR

Kimm Topping, Ed.M. (they/them/theirs) is an educator, writer, historian, and artist. They are the founder of Lavender Education, a national education program focused on celebrating LGBTQIA+ history, education, and youth leadership. From founding the first GSA in their hometown as a young person to now mentoring youth leaders and supporting educators, Kimm has always been passionate about building the confidence of others to lead social change.

For over ten years, Kimm has worked closely with schools and organizations on creating more inclusive, liberatory spaces for all LGBTQ+ youth to thrive. Prior to founding Lavender Education, Kimm managed the Safe Schools Program for LGBTQ Students in Massachusetts, a program of DESE. They currently lecture at the Harvard Graduate School of Education with specializations in gender, sexuality, and equity. In 2023, they received the inaugural In-Service Award from the Massachusetts Transgender Political Coalition recognizing their decade of service to Boston's trans community.

Generation Queer is Kimm's first full-length book. You can find Kimm on Instagram, @kimmwrites, or on their website, kimmtopping.com.

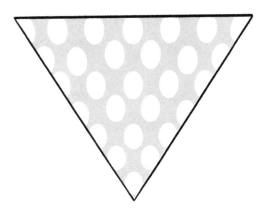

ABOUT THE ILLUSTRATOR

Anshika Khullar (they/them) is a nonbinary artist, video creator, and speaker based in Southampton, England. They are an ALA Stonewall Book Award winner, Renaissance Accelerated Reader Award winner, and CILIP Kate Greenaway Medal longlist nominee for their work on *The Black Flamingo* by Dean Atta. They also published a coloring and activity book, *Color Me Queer*, and focus their work on identity and culture, including queerness, body neutrality, South Asian diaspora experiences, immigration, mental illness, and trauma. Find their work online at aorists.com.

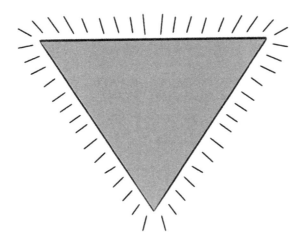

SOURCES

ACLU. "Mapping Attacks on LGBTQ Rights in US State Legislatures." ACLU, April 14, 2023, aclu.org/legislative-attacks-on-lgbtq-rights.

ACLU. "Grimm v. Gloucester County School Board." *American Civil Liberties Union*, ACLU, October 6, 2021, aclu.org/cases/grimm-v-gloucester -county-school-board.

Advocates for Trans Equality. "Know Your Rights: Schools." transequality.org /resources/know-your-rights-schools#:~:text=Title%20IX%20is%20a%20 federal,gender%2Drelated%20stereotypes%20or%20expectations.

Ahn, Kaylyn. "Bill Signing Speech HB5441." June 2022.

Ahn, Kaylyn. Zoom interview by the author. July 12, 2022.

Allen, Joshua. "Why Organizers Are Fighting to Center Black Trans Lives Right Now," *Vox*, June 18, 2020, vox.com/first-person/2020/6/18/21295610 /george-floyd-protests-black-trans-lives-dominique-fells-riah-milton.

Allen, Joshua. Zoom interview by the author. March 15, 2022.

Austin-Spooner, L. In-person interview by the author. October 6, 2019.

BAGLY. "Where We Came From." *Bagly, Inc.*, 2010, bagly.org/where-we -came-from.

Bailar, Schuyler. Zoom interview by the author. 2019.

Borge, Jonathan. "The Queer Black History of Rioting." *Refinery29*, June 15, 2020, refinery29.com/en-us/2020/06/9861317/first-pride-riots-history -black-lgbtq-blm.

Brogan, Mary Kate. "For Centuries, Two-Spirit People Had to Carry Out Native Traditions in Secret. Now, They're 'Making Their Own History.'" VCU News, April 25, 2022, news.vcu.edu/article/2022/04/for-centuries-two-spirit -people-had-to-carry-out-traditions-in-secret.

Bruesehoff, Rebekah. Zoom interview by the author. February 21, 2022.

Brundin, Jenny. "After Protests Over History Curriculum, School Board Tries to Compromise." NPR, October 3, 2014, npr.org/2014/10/03/353327302 /school-board-wants-civil-disorder-deemphasized-students-walk-out.

Burga, Solcyré. "How Four Trans Teens Threw the Prom of Their Dreams." *TIME*, May 22, 2023, time.com/6281601/trans-teens-prom-capitol.

Cassata, Ryan. Phone interview by the author. August 8, 2022.

Chanchan, Dehkontee. Phone interview by the author. October 12, 2019.

Couric, Katie, director. *Gender Revolution: A Journey with Katie Couric*. National Geographic Videos, TV Shows & Photos, Canada, February 6, 2017.

Cusolito, Alia. "State House Speech." We Are A State of Love: A Gathering of Visible Solidarity with LGBTQ Youth Event, March 31, 2022.

Dunn, Sara K. Zoom interview by the author. July 18, 2022.

Edelman, Marian Wright. "It's Hard to Be What You Can't See." Children's Defense Fund, August 21, 2015, childrensdefense.org/its-hard-to-be -what-you-cant-see.

Feinberg, Leslie. "Street Transvestite Action Revolutionaries found STAR House." *Workers World*, September 24, 2006, workers.org/2006/us/lavender-red-73.

"George Washington Goes Gay." *Growing Up Gay: A Youth Liberation Pamphlet*, no. 54 (Ann Arbor, MI: Youth Liberation Press, 1976), 20-24.

Gift, Reeves. Phone interview by the author. 2019.

GLBTQ Legal Advocates & Defenders. "The Right to Establish a GSA in Public Schools: A Basic Primer." January 2021, glad.org/wp-content/uploads /2021/02/GSA-Public-Schools.pdf.

Gleason, James. "LGBT History: The Lavender Scare." National LGBT Chamber of Commerce, October 3, 2017, nglcc.org/blog/lgbt-history-the -lavender-scare.

GLSEN Research Institute. "2021 National School Climate Survey." 2021, glsen .org/2021-national-school-climate-survey.

González, X. "A Young Activist's Advice: Vote, Shave Your Head and Cry Whenever You Need To." *New York Times*, October 5, 2018, nytimes .com/2018/10/05/opinion/sunday/emma-gonzalez-parkland.html.

Grant, JP. "Healthy Youth Act Rally Speech." Healthy Youth Act Coalition Rally, July 2022.

Grant, JP. Zoom interview by the author. July 20, 2022.

Grimm, Gavin. Zoom interview by the author. November 14, 2019.

Guillbeaux, Jess. Zoom interview by the author. March 22, 2022.

Haaland, Somah. Zoom interview by the author. April 11, 2022.

Harris, Sherenté Mishitashin. Zoom interview by the author. March 22, 2022.

Human Rights Campaign. "2018 LGBTQ Youth Report." 2017, hrc.org /resources/2018-lgbtq-youth-report.

Imani, Blair. Written interview. August 17, 2022.

interACT. "Intersex Definitions." February 19, 2021, interactadvocates.org /intersex-definitions.

Jha, Sameer. Zoom interview by the author. February 17, 2022.

Johnson, Dominique. "'This is Political!': Negotiating the Legacies of the First School-Based Gay Youth Group." *Children, Youth and Environments*, 2007, jstor.org/stable/10.7721/chilyoutenvi.17.2.0380.

Kirby, Jen. "The National School Walkout, Explained." *Vox*, March 14, 2018, vox .com/policy-and-politics/2018/3/13/17110044/national-school-walkout-day.

Lane, Stephen. *No Sanctuary: Teachers and the School Reform That Brought Gay Rights to the Masses.* ForeEdge, 2019.

Lee, Meg. Written interview. April 13, 2022.

Leins, Casey. "These States Require Schools to Teach LGBT History." *U.S. News*, August 14, 2019, usnews.com/news/best-states/articles/2019-08-14 /states-that-require-schools-to-teach-lgbt-history.

Lennon, Lillian. Phone interview by the author. October 12, 2019.

LGBT History Month. "Joseph Beam." 2013, lgbthistorymonth.com /joseph-beam?tab=biography.

Library of Congress. "1968: East Los Angeles Walkouts." *A Latinx Resource Guide: Civil Rights Cases and Events in the United States*, guides.loc.gov /latinx-civil-rights/east-la-walkouts.

Lockhart, P. R. "The Gun Reform Debate Has Largely Ignored Race. Black Students Made Sure the School Walkouts Didn't." *Vox*, March 14, 2018, vox.com/identities/2018/3/14/17120796/national-school-walkout-race -gun-violence-protests.

Macias-Gómez, Cyn. Zoom interview by the author. April 6, 2022.

McKenzie, Ella. Phone interview by the author. July 20, 2022.

McLean, Danielle. "A Trans Prom on the Capitol Lawn." *The Atlantic*, May 25, 2023, theatlantic.com/family/archive/2023/05/trans-youth-prom -washington-dc/674146.

Mixter, Win. "Pride Is a Protest." San Francisco Arts Commission, 2020, pride isaprotest.com/Info.

Montiel, Anya. "LGBTQIA+ Pride and Two-Spirit People." *Smithsonian Magazine*, June 23, 2021, smithsonianmag.com/blogs/national-museum-american -indian/2021/06/23/lgbtqia-pride-and-two-spirit-people.

Moricz, Zander. Written interview. August 12, 2022.

Morgan, Thaddeus. "How 19th-Century Drag Balls Evolved into House Balls, Birthplace of Voguing." A&E Television Networks, 2021, history.com/news /drag-balls-house-ballroom-voguing.

Morrison, Skyler. "Skyler Morrison's SB1165 Testimony." YouTube, March 9, 2022, youtube.com/watch?v=Nz96hnxjmRs.

Morrison, Skyler. Zoom interview by the author. August 3, 2022.

Morton, M. H., Samuels, G. M., Dworsky, A., & Patel, S. (2018). *Missed Opportunities: LGBTQ Youth Homelessness in America*. Chicago, IL: Chapin Hall at the University of Chicago.

Mota, Ashton. Zoom interview by the author. July 28, 2022.

Movement Advancement Project. "Equality Maps: Conversion Therapy Laws." August 4, 2022, lgbtmap.org/equality-maps/conversion_therapy.

Napoles, Desmond (Desi). Zoom interview by the author. March 3, 2022.

National Black Justice Coalition. "Inviting In Toolkit." November 30, 2020, nbjc.org/resource/inviting-in-toolkit.

Native Land Territories map. (2021). Native Land CA. native-land.ca.

Neal, Trinity. Zoom interview by the author. March 8, 2022.

New York Public Library. *The Stonewall Reader*. Penguin Classics, 2019.

Nugent, Alex. Written interview. August 21, 2024.

NYC LGBTQ. "Harvey Milk High School." *NYC LGBT Historic Sites Project*, 2016, nyclgbtsites.org/site/harvey-milk-high-school.

Ocamb, Karen. "Dr. Virginia Uribe, Project 10 Founder, Pioneer for LGBT Youth, Dies at 85." *Los Angeles Blade: LGBTQ News, Rights, Politics, Entertainment*, March 31, 2019, losangelesblade.com/2019/03/31/dr-virginia-uribe-project-10-founder-pioneer-for-lgbt-youth-dies-at-84.

O'Connor, Katherine. In-person interview by the author. October 6, 2019.

Out History: It's about Time! "Timeline: Asian American and Pacific Islander LGBTQ History, 1873–2022, August 7, 2020, outhistory.org/exhibits/show/asam-timeline/timeline.

PBS. "Kelli Peterson." pbs.org/outofthepast/past/p6/peterson.html.

Plaster, Joseph. "Living the Fantasy: A Brief History of Baltimore Ballroom." John Hopkins Sheridan Libraries, peabodyballroom.library.jhu.edu/home/ballroom-history.

Queer Youth Assemble Demands. Reproduced by permission of Queer Youth Assemble.

Silverman, Esmée. Zoom interview by the author. April 15, 2022.

Stanford Libraries. *Say Their Names*. Green Library Exhibit supporting the Black Lives Matter movement, exhibits.stanford.edu/saytheirnames.

Thurston, Isabella. "The History of Two-Spirit Folks." The Indigenous Foundation, theindigenousfoundation.org/articles/the-history-of-two-spirit-folks.

Truong, N. L., A. D. Zongrone, and J. G. Kosciw. "Erasure and Resilience: The Experiences of LGBTQ Students of Color: Black LGBTQ Youth in U.S. Schools," New York, GLSEN, glsen.org/sites/default/files/2020-06/Erasure -and-Resilience-Black-2020.pdf.

UT News. "Using Chosen Names Reduces Odds of Depression and Suicide in Transgender Youth." March 30, 2018, news.utexas.edu/2018/03/30 /name-use-matters-for-transgender-youths-mental-health.

Vaid-Menon, ALOK. Written interview. February 19, 2022.

Ventura, Anya. "The Radical History of the First Gay-Straight Alliance." *The Nation*, June 24, 2022, thenation.com/article/society/gay-liberation -high-school.

Venturiello, Michael. "Expressing Your Pride: LGBTQ+ Symbols Throughout History." Christopher Street Tours, Feburary 20, 2024, christopherstreettours .com/symbols.

Victory Institute. " LGBTQ Lawmakers in 16 States to Introduce Trans Refuge State Laws; Will Shield Trans Kids from Penalties When Seeking Gender- Affirming Care." May 3, 2022. victoryinstitute.org/news/lgbtq-lawmakers-in -16-states-to-introduce-trans-refuge-state-laws-will-shield-trans-kids-from -penalties-when-seeking-gender-affirming-care.

Washington, Bryan, and Ocean Vuong. "All the Ways to Be with Bryan Washington & Ocean Vuong." A24, December 21, 2020, a24films.com /notes/2020/12/all-the-ways-to-be-with-bryan-washington-ocean-vuong.

Waters, Emily. "Lesbian, Gay, Bisexual, Transgender, Queer, and HIV-Affected Hate Violence in 2016." AVP.org, 2017, avp.org/wp-content/uploads/2017/06/NCAVP_2016HateViolence_REPORT.pdf.

Weaver, Josh. "New Poll Illustrates the Impacts of Social & Political Issues on LGBTQ Youth." The Trevor Project, January 10, 2022, thetrevorproject.org/blog/new-poll-illustrates-the-impacts-of-social-political-issues-on-lgbtq-youth.

Willis, Raquel. "How Miss Major Helped Spark the Modern Trans Movement." Them, March 8, 2018, them.us/story/transvisionaries-miss-major.

Wilson, Rodney. "The Early History of LGBTQ+ History Month." Lecture at Southeast Missouri State, October 2019, youtube.com/watch?v=cKERNHzydZY.

Wrobi, Mari. Zoom interview by the author. February 18, 2022.

Yearwood, Andraya. Written interview. July 27, 2022.

Yurcaba, Jo. "Different Fight, 'Same Goal': How the Black Freedom Movement Inspired Early Gay Activists." NBCNews.com, NBCUniversal News Group, February 28, 2021, nbcnews.com/feature/nbc-out/different-fight-same-goal-how-black-freedom-movement-inspired-early-n1259072.

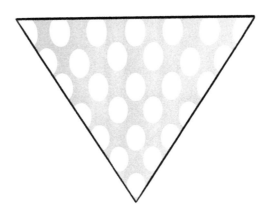